PHYSIOLOGICAL PSYCHOLOGY

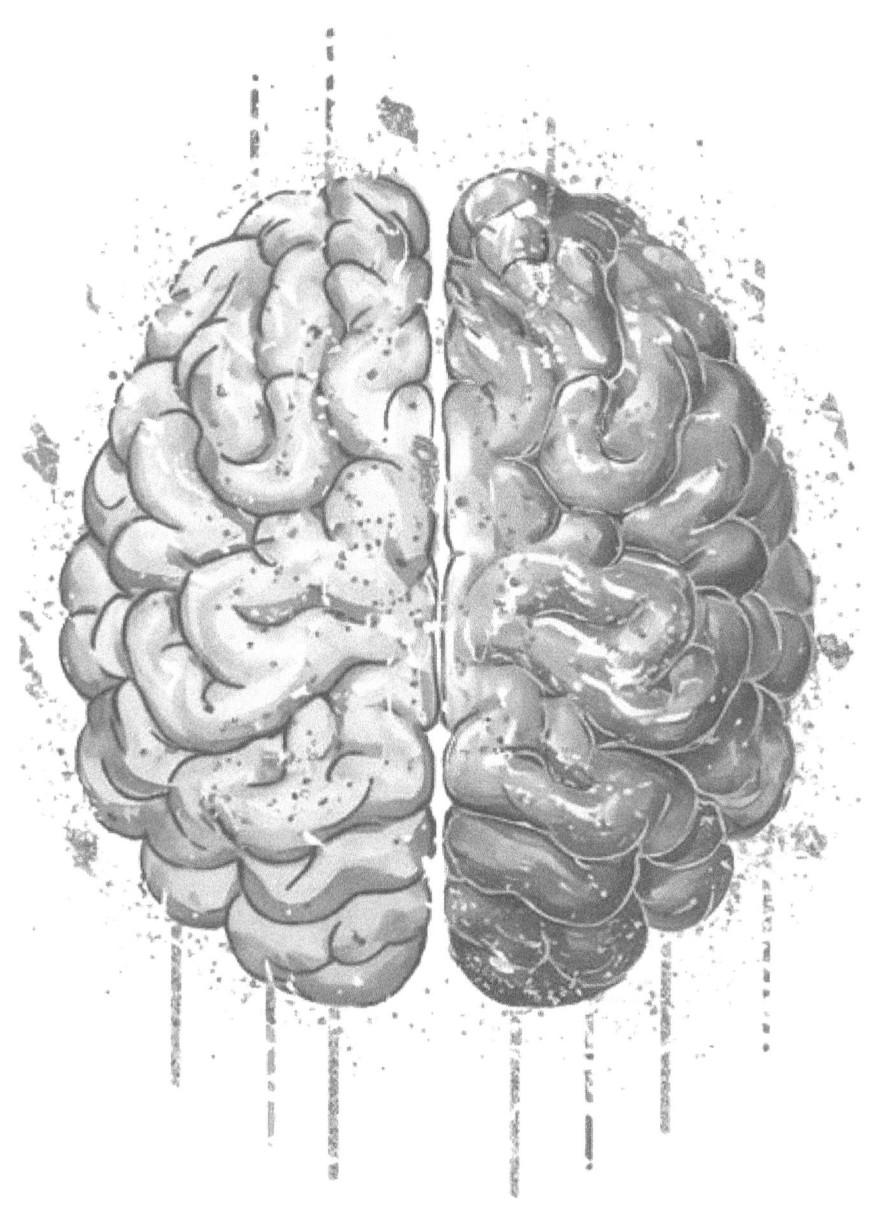

Jasmeet Kaur

Ph.D Scholar

M.Sc. Psychology (Clinical)

NET Qualified / GATE Qualified (AIR: 198)

Author's Note & Acknowledgements

This book, like its sister volumes, is offered in goodwill, sincerity, and deep concern for my students of past, present, and future. It is not just a compilation of academic knowledge, but a reflection of care, lived experiences, and the heart I carry into every classroom.

I dedicate this work to Akaal-purakh, the timeless divine, whose grace flows through every word and every intention. I acknowledge, with folded hands, the channel of blessings that comes through my parents, whose unwavering support and faith have shaped both my life and my abilities.

"Sab Gobind Hai, Gobind Bin Nahi Koye."
Everything is God; there is nothing that is not divine.

This is more than a textbook. It is a heartfelt academic and spiritual offering—an effort to hold, guide, and uplift, especially for those navigating the challenging terrain of Biopsychology.

Designed specifically for Master's students, this book closely follows the syllabus of Punjabi University, Patiala. Future editions may expand to integrate updated research, broader curriculum mappings, and refined understanding as we all continue to grow in the journey of knowledge.

With humility and strength.
Always,

Jasmeet Kaur

INDEX

ORIGIN OF PHYSIOLOGICAL PSYCHOLOGY

(and its renaming as Biopsychology)

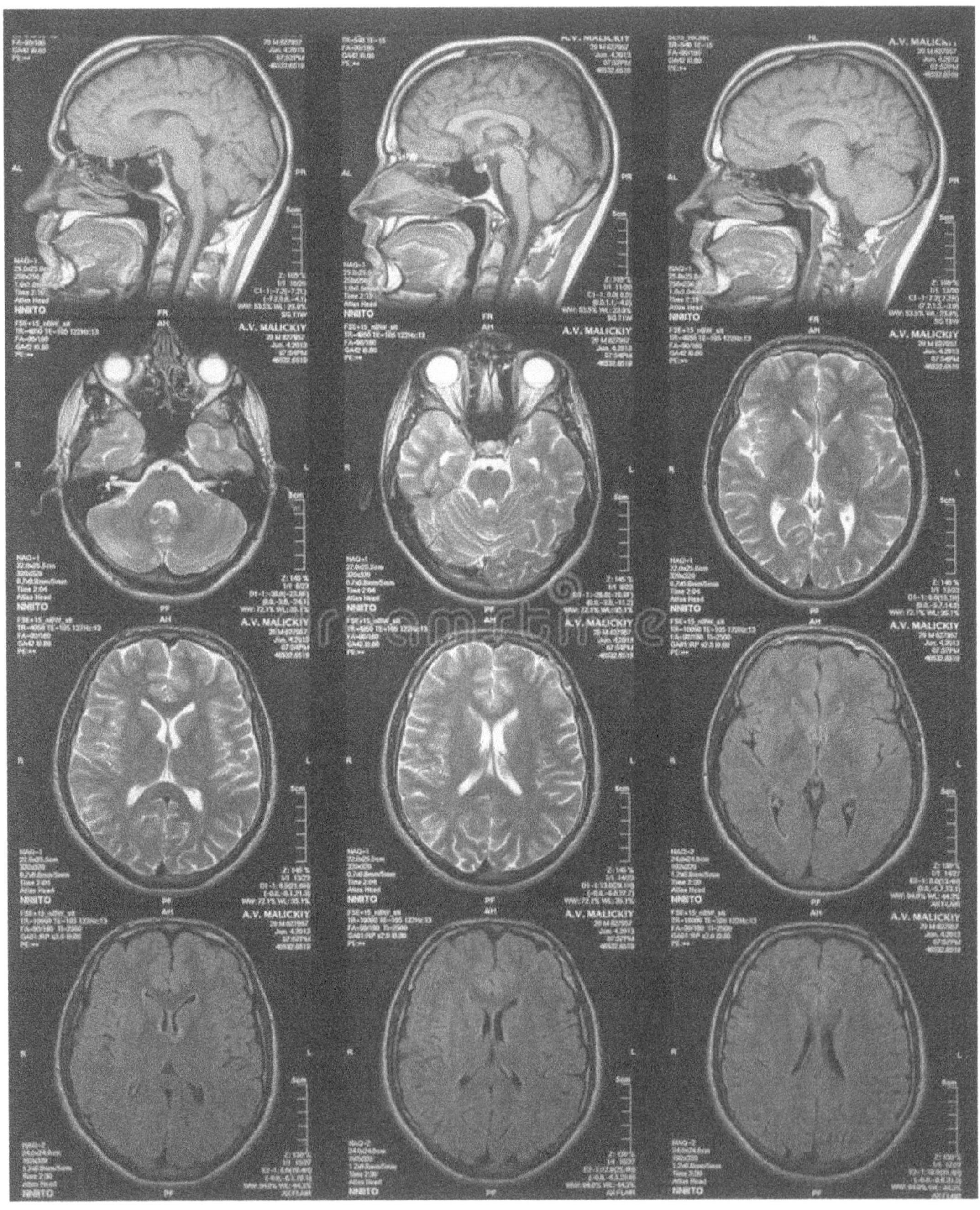

ORIGIN OF PHYSIOLOGICAL PSYCHOLOGY

Physiological psychology is a branch of psychology that explores the biological underpinnings of behaviour, emotions, perception, and cognition. It focuses primarily on how the brain, nervous system, endocrine system, and other bodily mechanisms influence psychological processes.

- ◇ 1. Philosophical Foundations (Ancient to 17th Century)

  - In ancient Greece, philosophers like Hippocrates and Galen proposed that the brain—not the heart—was the centre of mental activity.

  - Plato and Aristotle debated the mind-body problem. Aristotle believed in the heart as the seat of thought, while Plato emphasized reason residing in the brain.

  - René Descartes (17th century) introduced mind-body dualism, claiming the mind and body are separate but interact through the pineal gland. Though flawed, this dualism spurred scientific interest in biological processes behind behaviour.

- ◇ 2. Emergence as a Scientific Field (18th–19th Century)

  - With the rise of empirical science, thinkers like Luigi Galvani (electricity and frog legs) demonstrated that electrical impulses could initiate muscle movement.

  - Johannes Müller and Charles Bell contributed to the doctrine of specific nerve energies.

  - Paul Broca and Carl Wernicke localized language functions in specific brain areas, laying foundations for neuropsychology.

  - Gustav Fechner developed psychophysics to study how physical stimuli relate to psychological experiences.

  - Wilhelm Wundt established the first psychology lab in 1879, using experimental methods to study sensation and reaction times, integrating physiological techniques into psychological research.

◇ 3. Modern Developments (20th–21st Century)

- The 20th century saw the evolution of neurophysiology, behavioural neuroscience, neuropsychology, and cognitive neuroscience.

- Tools like EEG, MRI, PET, and fMRI allowed real-time study of brain activity during cognitive and emotional tasks.

- Studies of patients with brain lesions (e.g., Phineas Gage) helped link brain regions to behaviour and personality.

- Hormonal studies and neurochemical research helped understand mood, motivation, addiction, stress, and disorders like schizophrenia or depression.

SCOPE OF PHYSIOLOGICAL PSYCHOLOGY

Physiological psychology spans a wide spectrum of research and application. Its scope includes:

1. Brain–Behaviour Relationships:
   - Studies how specific areas of the brain control motor functions, decision-making, memory, or emotions.

2. Nervous System Functioning:
   - Covers central and peripheral nervous systems, spinal reflexes, and neurotransmission processes.

3. Hormonal Influences:
   - Explores how endocrine glands and hormones like cortisol, dopamine, estrogen, and testosterone affect mood, stress, aggression, and sexual behaviour.

4. Sensation and Perception:
   - Analyzes how stimuli from the environment are processed by sensory organs and interpreted in the brain (e.g., visual cortex, auditory cortex).

5. Emotions and Motivation:
   - Investigates the limbic system's role in emotion and the hypothalamus' control of hunger, thirst, or reward-seeking behaviour.

6. Sleep and Biological Rhythms:

    - Examines circadian rhythms, sleep cycles (REM, non-REM), and disorders like insomnia or narcolepsy.

7. Learning and Memory:

    - Studies hippocampus, amygdala, and neurotransmitters in encoding, storage, and retrieval of memories.

8. Psychopharmacology:

    - Explores how psychoactive drugs affect brain chemistry and psychological functioning (used in treating mental illness).

9. Brain Damage and Rehabilitation:

    - Helps in designing rehabilitation strategies after strokes, injuries, or degenerative diseases.

10. Evolutionary and Developmental Aspects:

    - Understands how evolutionary biology shaped brain structures and how brain development affects behaviour across the lifespan.

RELATION OF PHYSIOLOGICAL PSYCHOLOGY TO OTHER DISCIPLINES

Physiological psychology is inherently interdisciplinary. It draws from, and contributes to, several fields:

1. Neuroscience:

    - A foundational overlap. While neuroscience is broader (including cellular and molecular levels), physiological psychology focuses on how these biological processes influence behaviour and cognition.

2. Medicine and Neurology:

    - Helps understand brain-based disorders such as epilepsy, Parkinson's disease, Alzheimer's, and multiple sclerosis.

    - Clinical neurologists use physiological psychology principles to diagnose and treat neurological disorders.

3. Psychiatry:

    - Supports diagnosis and treatment of mental disorders like depression, bipolar disorder, anxiety, and schizophrenia through an understanding of neurotransmitters, brain regions, and drug mechanisms.

4. Cognitive Psychology:

    - Merges with physiological psychology to form cognitive neuroscience, which studies the neural basis of memory, attention, decision-making, and consciousness.

5. Behavioural Psychology:

    - Reinforced early on by animal studies (like Pavlov's and Skinner's), physiological psychology studies conditioned responses in terms of neural circuitry.

6. Endocrinology:

    - Examines hormonal mechanisms of stress, puberty, sexual behaviour, and endocrine disorders affecting behaviour.

7. Genetics and Epigenetics:

    - Studies how genetic predispositions and gene–environment interactions influence personality, intelligence, and vulnerability to mental illness.

8. Evolutionary Psychology:

    - Integrates brain evolution and adaptive behaviours, focusing on survival and reproductive fitness in relation to brain structures and functions.

9. Developmental Psychology:

    - Studies how brain maturation relates to cognitive, emotional, and motor development in infants, children, and adolescents.

10. Psychopharmacology:

    - A specialized field that examines how substances like antidepressants, antipsychotics, or stimulants alter neurotransmission and behaviour.

11. Artificial Intelligence and Robotics:

    - Inspired by neural network functioning, helping simulate cognition and adaptive behaviour in machines.

Physiological psychology bridges the gap between biology and psychology. It allows us to understand how brain and body processes influence the way we think, feel, and act. As psychology becomes increasingly evidence-based and neurobiological in orientation, physiological psychology plays a pivotal role in advancing research, diagnostics, and therapeutic interventions in both clinical and academic settings.

RESEARCH METHODS:

1. Stimulation

- **Definition**: Stimulation involves artificially activating specific areas of the brain using external methods to observe their impact on behaviour, sensation, or movement.

- **Methods of Stimulation**:

    - **Electrical Stimulation**: Delivering small electrical currents through electrodes to specific brain regions.

    - **Chemical Stimulation**: Introducing neurotransmitters or other chemical agents to stimulate brain regions.

    - **Magnetic Stimulation**: Using Transcranial Magnetic Stimulation (TMS) to modulate brain activity non-invasively.

- **Applications**:

    - Mapping brain functions (e.g., motor cortex stimulation leads to muscle movements).

    - Investigating sensory areas (e.g., visual or auditory cortex stimulation to evoke sensations).

    - Studying the effects of stimulation in treating conditions like depression (TMS is used for treatment).

- **Advantages**:

    - Provides insights into brain function by directly manipulating brain regions.

    - Can be used in both animal models and humans (e.g., during brain surgery).

- **Limitations**:

    - Effects are short-term and may not reflect real-world brain activity.

- o Can be invasive or limited to specific contexts (e.g., neurosurgery).

2. Ablation (Lesion Method)

- **Definition**: Ablation involves the deliberate destruction or removal of specific brain tissue to study the resulting behavioural changes and understand the function of that brain region.

- **Methods of Ablation**:

  - o **Surgical Lesions**: Removing or damaging tissue from specific brain areas in animals (e.g., hippocampus removal in rats).

  - o **Chemical Lesions**: Injecting chemicals to destroy specific neurons in certain regions.

  - o **Radiofrequency Lesions**: Using high-frequency electrical currents to burn specific brain areas.

- **Applications**:

  - o Helps understand the role of brain areas in cognitive processes, memory, emotions, and motor control.

  - o Important for studies on brain localization, such as Broca's and Wernicke's areas for language.

- **Advantages**:

  - o Provides direct evidence of the causal relationship between brain regions and behaviour.

  - o Essential for studying the neural basis of learning, memory, and emotions.

- **Limitations**:

  - o Ethical concerns limit its use in humans (except in medical conditions like epilepsy treatment).

  - o The damage can be irreversible, leading to significant behavioural changes.

3. Neuropsychological Testing

- **Definition**: Neuropsychological testing involves the use of structured tasks and assessments to evaluate cognitive, emotional, and motor functions linked to brain activity. These tests help identify brain dysfunction and changes.

- **Methods of Neuropsychological Testing**:

  - **Cognitive Tests**: Assessments of memory, attention, reasoning, and executive functions (e.g., Wisconsin Card Sorting Test, Stroop Test).

  - **Emotional and Personality Assessments**: Measure emotional regulation and personality traits using scales like the Beck Depression Inventory.

  - **Motor Function Tests**: Assess motor control and coordination (e.g., Finger Tapping Test).

- **Applications**:

  - Diagnosing brain damage, neurological disorders, or cognitive decline (e.g., Alzheimer's disease).

  - Tracking changes in cognitive abilities over time, often used in clinical settings for rehabilitation.

  - Assessing the effects of brain injuries, strokes, or neurodegenerative diseases.

- **Advantages**:

  - Non-invasive and provides detailed, individualized assessments.

  - Can be used to detect subtle cognitive and emotional changes before structural changes are visible.

- **Limitations**:

  - May not capture all brain functions or provide a complete picture of complex cognitive processes.

  - Can be influenced by external factors like education, culture, and emotional state.

BRAIN IMAGING TECHNIQUES:

1. Electroconvulsive Therapy (ECT)

- **Definition**: Electroconvulsive Therapy (ECT) is a brain treatment method that involves applying electrical currents to the brain to induce a controlled seizure. It is primarily used to treat severe psychiatric disorders such as depression, bipolar disorder, and schizophrenia.

- **Mechanism**:

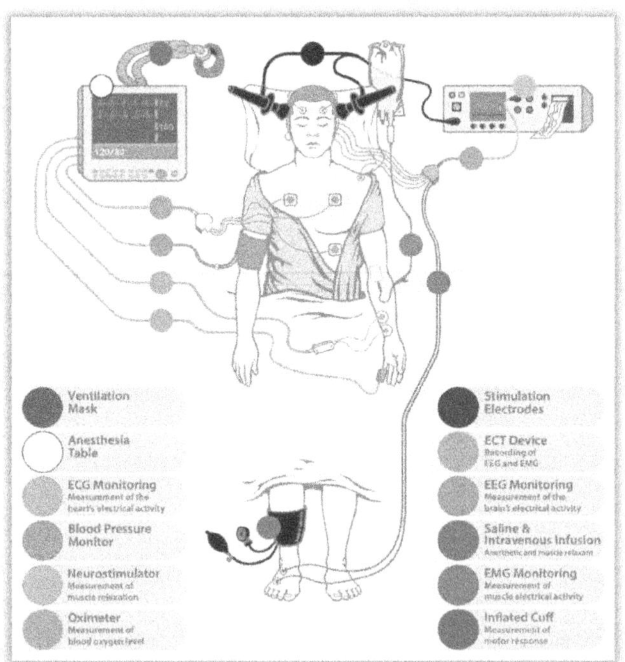

  - Electrodes are placed on the scalp, and a brief electrical pulse is sent to the brain to trigger a controlled seizure.

  - The electrical activity stimulates neurotransmitter release, leading to changes in brain chemistry.

- **Applications**:

  - **Psychiatric Treatment**: ECT is used to treat conditions that do not respond to medications, including severe depression, mania, and some forms of schizophrenia.

  - **Research Tool**: Although not typically used as a diagnostic imaging technique, ECT can be part of brain research on electrical brain stimulation and its effects on mood and cognition.

- o **Advantages**:

- o Highly effective for treatment-resistant psychiatric disorders.

- o Rapid onset of therapeutic effects, especially in severe cases of depression.

- **Limitations**:

- o Side effects include memory loss, confusion, and temporary cognitive impairments.

- o The exact mechanism of action is not fully understood, though it is believed to modulate brain chemistry.

- o Ethical concerns regarding informed consent and its use in vulnerable populations.

- **Note**: ECT is not primarily an imaging tool, but its impact on brain activity is often studied using **EEG** or brain imaging techniques (e.g., fMRI) to assess changes in brain functioning post-treatment.

2. Computerized Axial Tomography (CAT)

- **Definition**: Computerized Axial Tomography (CAT), also known as CT (Computed Tomography), is a non-invasive brain imaging technique that uses X-rays to create detailed cross-sectional images (slices) of the brain.

- **Mechanism**:

- o A rotating X-ray beam scans the brain from multiple angles.

- o The data is processed by a computer to generate detailed 3D images of the brain's structure.

- o Contrast dyes may be injected into the bloodstream to enhance the visibility of certain brain areas or abnormalities.

- **Applications**:

  o **Brain Structure Analysis**: CAT scans provide high-resolution images of brain structures, enabling the detection of tumours, lesions, strokes, and other structural abnormalities.

  o **Trauma Assessment**: Used to assess head injuries or brain haemorrhages and to guide surgical interventions.

  o **Pre-surgical Planning**: Helps in mapping brain regions before surgery, particularly in epilepsy treatment or tumour removal.

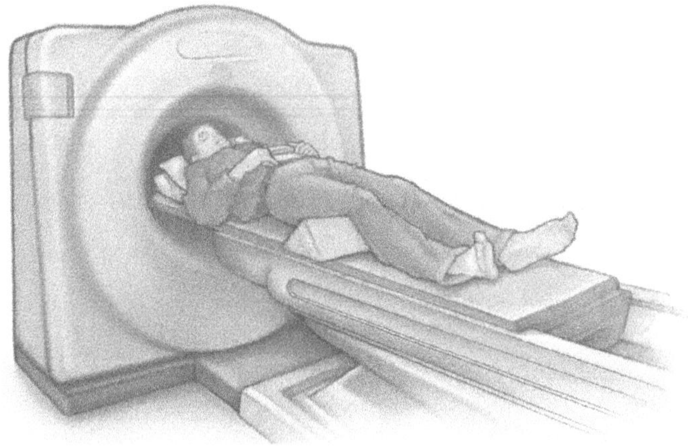

- **Advantages**:

  o Quick and widely available.

  o Non-invasive and provides clear structural images.

  o Can detect a wide range of brain abnormalities, such as brain tumors, bleeds, or atrophy.

- **Limitations**:

  o Involves exposure to X-rays, which can be harmful in excessive amounts.

  o Lower resolution compared to MRI (Magnetic Resonance Imaging) in soft tissue detail.

  o Not effective for detecting certain functional abnormalities (e.g., metabolic changes).

3. Superconducting Quantum Interference Device (SQUID)

- **Definition**: The Superconducting Quantum Interference Device (SQUID) is a highly sensitive magnetometer used to measure the faint magnetic fields generated by neural activity in the brain. This technique is known as **Magnetoencephalography (MEG)**.

- **Mechanism**:

  o SQUID detects the magnetic fields produced by neuronal electrical activity, specifically the synchronous firing of neurons.

  o It uses superconducting materials and quantum interference to measure extremely weak magnetic fields (on the scale of femtoteslas).

  o The detected magnetic signals are then analyzed to map brain activity in real-time.

- **Applications**:

  o **Functional Brain Mapping**: SQUID is used for mapping brain regions involved in motor, sensory, language, and cognitive functions.

  o **Epilepsy Localization**: Helps locate the source of epileptic seizures by detecting abnormal magnetic fields associated with seizure activity.

  o **Research**: Used to study brain activity in both normal and pathological conditions, offering insights into cognitive processes, neural oscillations, and sensory processing.

  o **Pre-surgical Planning**: Often used to map sensory or motor regions before brain surgery, especially in patients with epilepsy.

- **Advantages**:

  o Non-invasive and provides real-time data on brain activity.

  o Superior temporal resolution (on the millisecond scale) compared to other imaging methods like fMRI.

  o Allows direct measurement of neuronal activity, unlike indirect methods (e.g., blood flow in fMRI).

- **Limitations**:

- o   Extremely expensive and not widely available.

- o   The technique is highly sensitive to environmental magnetic noise, requiring a magnetically shielded room.

- o   Limited spatial resolution compared to other imaging methods like fMRI and PET scans.

Summary :

Technique	Main Purpose	Strengths	Limitations
ECT (Electroconvulsive Therapy)	Used as a treatment for psychiatric disorders, primarily depression	Rapid therapeutic effects, effective for treatment-resistant cases	Side effects include memory loss and cognitive impairment
CAT (Computerized Axial Tomography)	Provides structural brain images using X-rays	Quick, non-invasive, detects a range of abnormalities	Exposure to X-rays, lower resolution than MRI
SQUID (Superconducting Quantum Interference Device)	Measures brain activity by detecting magnetic fields from neural activity (MEG)	Real-time data with high temporal resolution, non-invasive	Expensive, requires magnetic shielding, limited spatial resolution

NEURON- ITS STRUCTURE AND FUNCTION

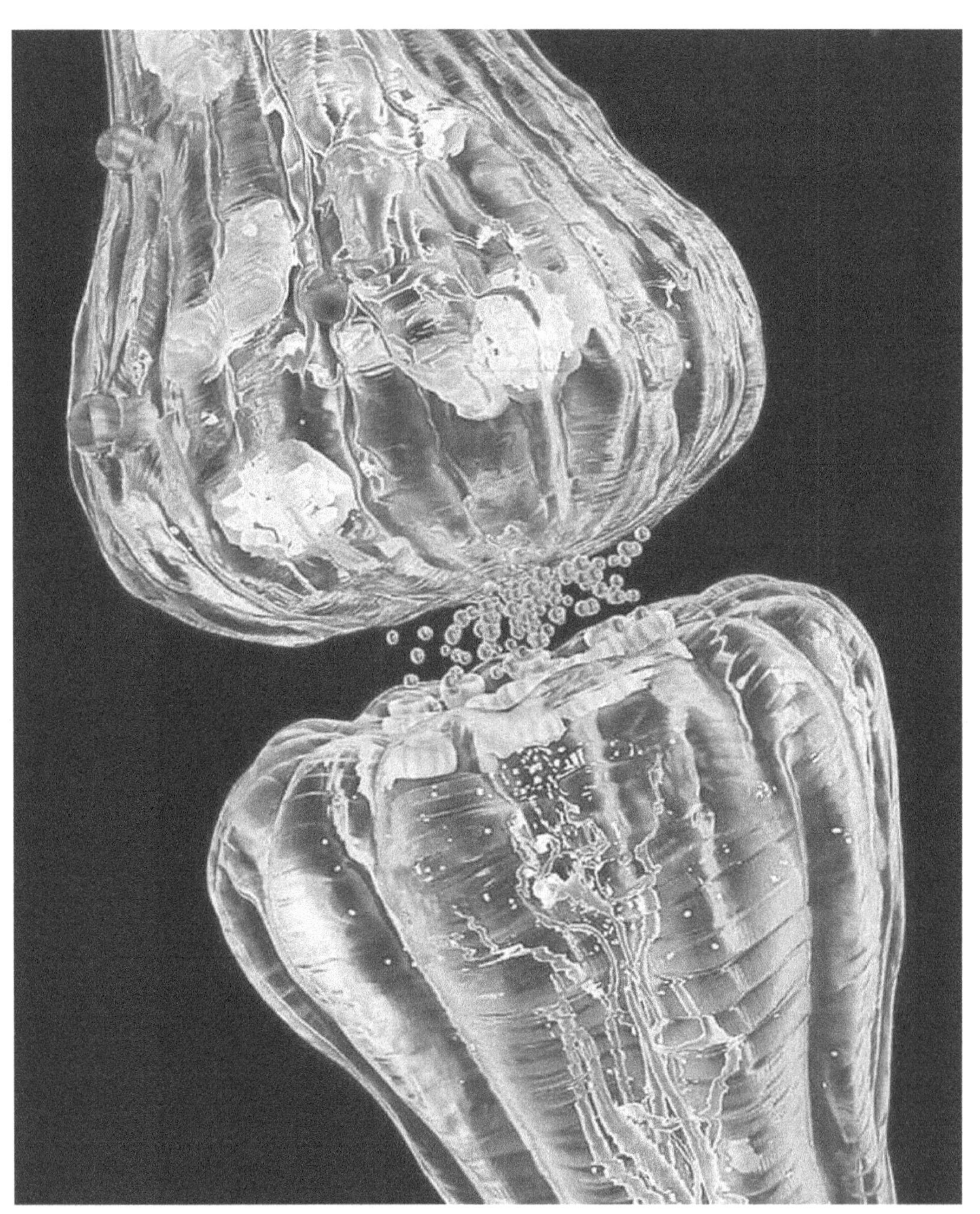

NEURON

A **neuron** is the fundamental unit of the nervous system, responsible for receiving, processing, and transmitting information through electrical and chemical signals.

Structure of a Neuron

A neuron is a highly specialized cell designed to transmit electrical and chemical signals. It consists of the following major structures:

Structure of a Neuron

A neuron consists of several key components, each with specific functions:

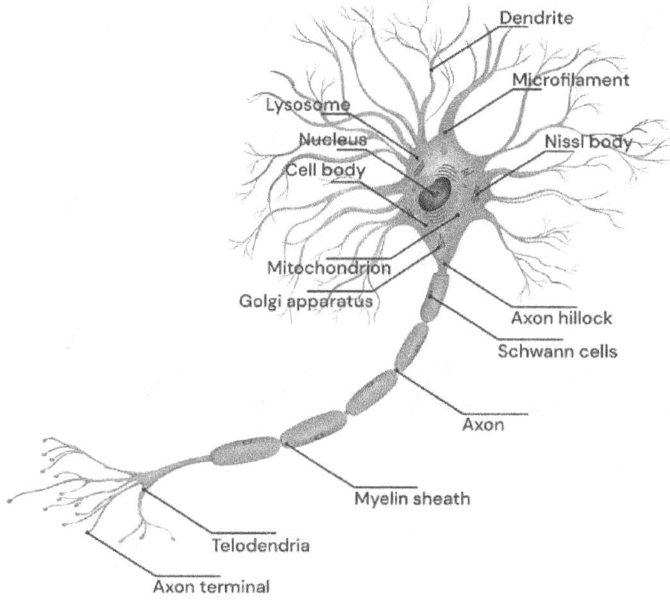

1. **Cell Body (Soma)**

o   The cell body contains the **nucleus**, which houses genetic material (DNA).

o   It is responsible for metabolic activities and the synthesis of neurotransmitters.

o   The soma integrates incoming signals from dendrites and generates appropriate responses.

2. **Dendrites**

o   These are branch-like structures extending from the soma.

o   Their primary function is to receive signals from other neurons and transmit them to the cell body.

o   Dendrites contain receptors for neurotransmitters released by neighboring neurons.

3. **Axon**

- A long, tube-like structure that carries electrical impulses away from the cell body toward other neurons or effectors (muscles or glands).

- The axon can vary in length, from a few micrometers to over a meter (e.g., in spinal cord neurons).

- Axons are covered with the **myelin sheath** in many neurons, which speeds up signal transmission.

4. **Myelin Sheath**

- A fatty, insulating layer covering the axon, composed of **Schwann cells (in the peripheral nervous system)** or **oligodendrocytes (in the central nervous system)**.

- It increases the speed of nerve impulse conduction through **saltatory conduction**, where impulses jump between gaps called **Nodes of Ranvier**.

5. **Nodes of Ranvier**

- Small gaps between sections of the myelin sheath.

- These nodes allow for rapid signal transmission by enabling action potentials to jump from one node to another.

6. **Axon Terminals (Terminal Buttons)**

- The endpoints of the axon that contain **synaptic vesicles** filled with neurotransmitters.

- When an action potential reaches the terminals, neurotransmitters are released into the **synaptic cleft**, allowing communication between neurons.

7. **Synapse (Synaptic Cleft)**

- The microscopic gap between the axon terminal of one neuron and the dendrite of another.

- Neurotransmitters cross this gap to transmit signals from one neuron to the next.

Types of Neurons

Neurons can be classified into different types based on their **structure** (morphology) and **function** (role in the nervous system). This classification helps in understanding how information is transmitted and processed within the brain and body.

A. Based on Structure

The structural classification of neurons is determined by the number of extensions (processes) arising from the cell body.

1. Unipolar Neurons (Pseudounipolar Neurons)

- Have a single extension from the cell body, which splits into two branches:

  - One branch functions as a dendrite (receives signals).

  - The other acts as an axon (sends signals).

- Found primarily in sensory neurons of the peripheral nervous system (PNS), such as those in the dorsal root ganglia.

- **Function:** Transmit sensory information (touch, pain, temperature) from the body to the spinal cord.

2. Bipolar Neurons

- Have two extensions:

  - One dendrite that receives signals.

  - One axon that transmits signals.

- Found in specialized sensory organs like the retina (eye), olfactory bulb (smell), and inner ear (hearing & balance).

- **Function:** Process sensory information in vision, smell, and hearing.

3. Multipolar Neurons

- Have multiple dendrites and a single axon.

- The most common type of neuron in the central nervous system (CNS).

- **Examples:**

  o   Motor neurons that control muscle movement.

  o   Interneurons that connect different neurons in the brain and spinal cord.

- **Function:** Process and integrate information, facilitate communication between neurons, and control voluntary and involuntary actions.

4. Anaxonic Neurons

- Do not have a distinct axon; all extensions appear similar.

- Found in the brain and retina.

- **Function:** Involved in processing complex neural networks, particularly in visual processing.

- **B.   Types of Neurons Based on Function**

The functional classification of neurons is based on their role in receiving, processing, and transmitting information.

1. Sensory Neurons (Afferent Neurons)

- Transmit signals from sensory receptors (e.g., skin, eyes, ears) to the central nervous system (CNS: brain and spinal cord).

- Mostly unipolar or bipolar in structure.

- Example: Neurons in the skin detecting temperature and pain, sending signals to the spinal cord and brain.

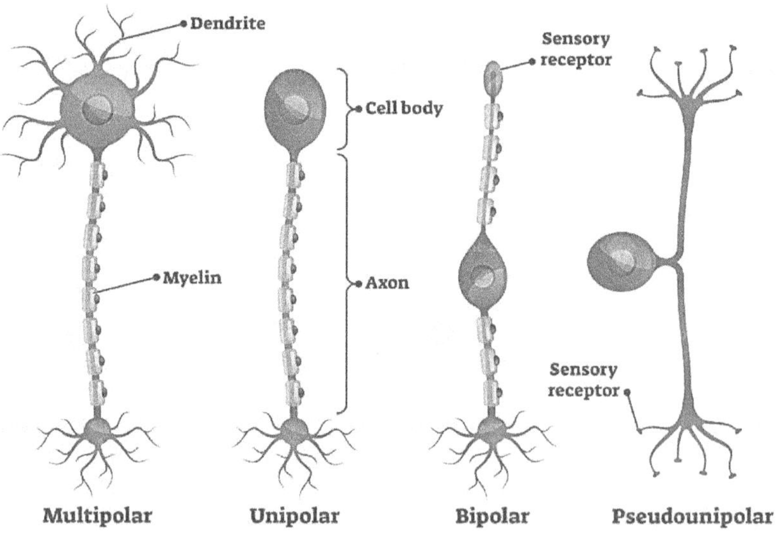

- Function: Carry sensory information such as touch, temperature, pain, sound, and light to the CNS.

2. Motor Neurons (Efferent Neurons)

- Carry signals from the CNS to muscles and glands.

- Mostly multipolar in structure.

- Example: Neurons that stimulate muscle contraction during movement.

- Function: Control voluntary and involuntary movements (e.g., reflexes, muscle contractions, gland secretions).

3. Interneurons (Association Neurons)

- Found entirely within the CNS (brain and spinal cord).

- Mostly multipolar in structure.

- **Function:**

  ○ Process information and relay signals between sensory and motor neurons.

  ○ Play a crucial role in reflex actions and higher cognitive functions (e.g., thinking, learning, memory).

- **Example:** Interneurons in the spinal cord mediate reflexes, bypassing the brain to produce fast responses to stimuli.

Functions of a Neuron

Neurons function through **electrical and chemical signaling** in three main stages:

1. Receiving Signals (Input Stage)

- Neurons receive signals through dendrites in the form of **excitatory** or **inhibitory** neurotransmitters.

- These signals alter the **membrane potential**, determining whether the neuron will fire an action potential.

2. Processing and Transmission of Signals

- If the combined signals at the **axon hillock** (junction of soma and axon) reach the **threshold potential**, an **action potential** is generated.

- The action potential propagates along the axon toward the terminals.

3. Communication at the Synapse (Output Stage)

- When the action potential reaches the axon terminals, **neurotransmitters** are released into the synapse.

- These neurotransmitters bind to receptors on the next neuron, triggering a response (either excitatory or inhibitory).

- The process is terminated by **reuptake**, **enzymatic breakdown**, or **diffusion** of neurotransmitters.

Role of Neurons in Psychological Disorders

According to Carlson's book, abnormal neuronal function is linked to mental disorders such as:

- **Depression**: Low levels of serotonin and dopamine.

- **Schizophrenia**: Excess dopamine activity.

- **Anxiety Disorders**: Overactive neural circuits in the amygdala.

- **Alzheimer's Disease**: Degeneration of acetylcholine-producing neurons.

SUPPORTING CELLS

Neurons are the primary functional units of the nervous system, but they **cannot function alone**. They require support from specialized **glial cells**, which provide structural support, insulation, immune defense, and help in the maintenance of the neuronal environment. These **non-neuronal cells** play a critical role in the health and efficiency of neural communication.

Types of Supporting Cells of Neurons

Supporting cells are broadly categorized into **glial cells** (neuroglia) found in the **central nervous system (CNS)** and **Schwann cells** found in the **peripheral nervous system (PNS)**.

1. Glial Cells (Neuroglia) in the Central Nervous System (CNS)

The **CNS (brain and spinal cord)** contains four major types of glial cells:

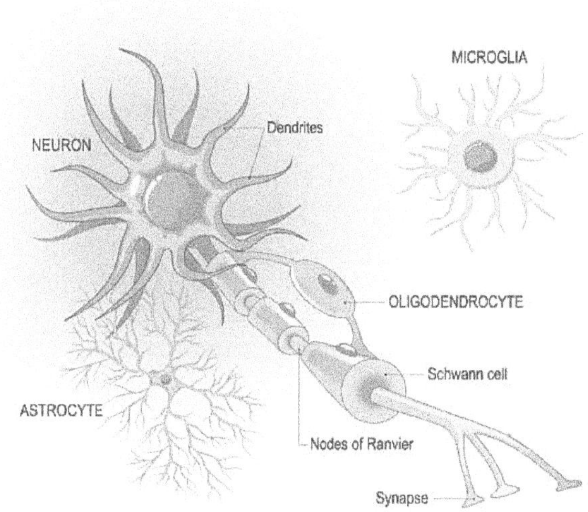

1. **Astrocytes**

2. **Oligodendrocytes**

3. **Microglia**

4. **Ependymal Cells** (not often discussed, but they help produce cerebrospinal fluid)

(i) Astrocytes: The Star-Shaped Support Cells

-   **Structure**: Large, star-shaped glial cells.

-   **Function**:

    -   **Blood-Brain Barrier (BBB)**: Astrocytes form a barrier that controls the movement of substances between the blood and the brain.

    -   **Nutrient Transport**: Provide nutrients (e.g., glucose) to neurons.

    -   **Regulation of Neurotransmitters**: Absorb excess neurotransmitters like glutamate to prevent overstimulation.

    -   **Repair and Scar Formation**: In case of brain injury, astrocytes form a protective scar to prevent further damage.

Clinical Relevance:

- Astrocyte dysfunction is linked to **neurodegenerative diseases** like **Alzheimer's disease** (accumulation of toxic proteins).

(ii) Oligodendrocytes: The Myelin Producers of the CNS

- **Structure**: Small glial cells with multiple extensions, wrapping around several axons.

- **Function**:

    o Produce **myelin** (a fatty insulating sheath) in the CNS.

    o Increase the **speed of nerve impulse conduction** (saltatory conduction).

    o Provide **metabolic support** to neurons.

(iii) Microglia: The Immune Cells of the Brain

- **Structure**: Small, mobile, phagocytic cells.

- **Function**:

    o Act as **the brain's immune system** by removing dead cells and pathogens.

    o Secrete **inflammatory molecules** to fight infections.

    o Help in **synaptic pruning** (removal of weak neuronal connections to optimize brain function).

- **Clinical Relevance**:

    o Overactive microglia contribute to **neuroinflammation**, seen in disorders like **Parkinson's disease** and **Alzheimer's disease**.

2. Supporting Cells in the Peripheral Nervous System (PNS)

The **PNS (nerves outside the brain and spinal cord)** has two major types of support cells:

(iv) Schwann Cells: Myelin Sheath Producers of the PNS

- **Structure**: Wrap around a single axon in the PNS.

- **Function**:

    - Produce **myelin** to insulate axons in the PNS.

    - **Aid in nerve regeneration** by guiding axonal regrowth after injury.

- **Clinical Relevance**:

    - Damage to Schwann cells can cause **peripheral neuropathies**, leading to sensory and motor deficits (e.g., in **Guillain-Barré syndrome**).

Glial cells and Schwann cells are **essential for neuron survival and function**. They provide **structural support, myelin insulation, immune defense, and help regulate the neural environment**. Dysfunction of these cells is linked to serious neurological diseases like **multiple sclerosis, Alzheimer's, Parkinson's, and peripheral neuropathies**

CONDUCTION OF A NERVE IMPULSE

The **conduction of a nerve impulse** refers to the transmission of electrical signals along the neuron, allowing communication between different parts of the nervous system. This process takes place in the form of **electrical and chemical signaling mechanisms**, including action potentials, ion channels, and synaptic transmission.

Phases of Nerve Impulse Conduction

The conduction of a nerve impulse occurs in two main stages:

1. **Electrical conduction (within the neuron)** → Action Potential

2. **Chemical transmission (between neurons)** → Synaptic Transmission

1. **Electrical Conduction: Action Potential**

Resting Potential (-70mV) --->   Depolarization (+40mV) --->   Repolarization (-70mV)

(Na+/K+ pump maintains charge)   (Na+ enters inside cell)   (K+ exits cell inside)

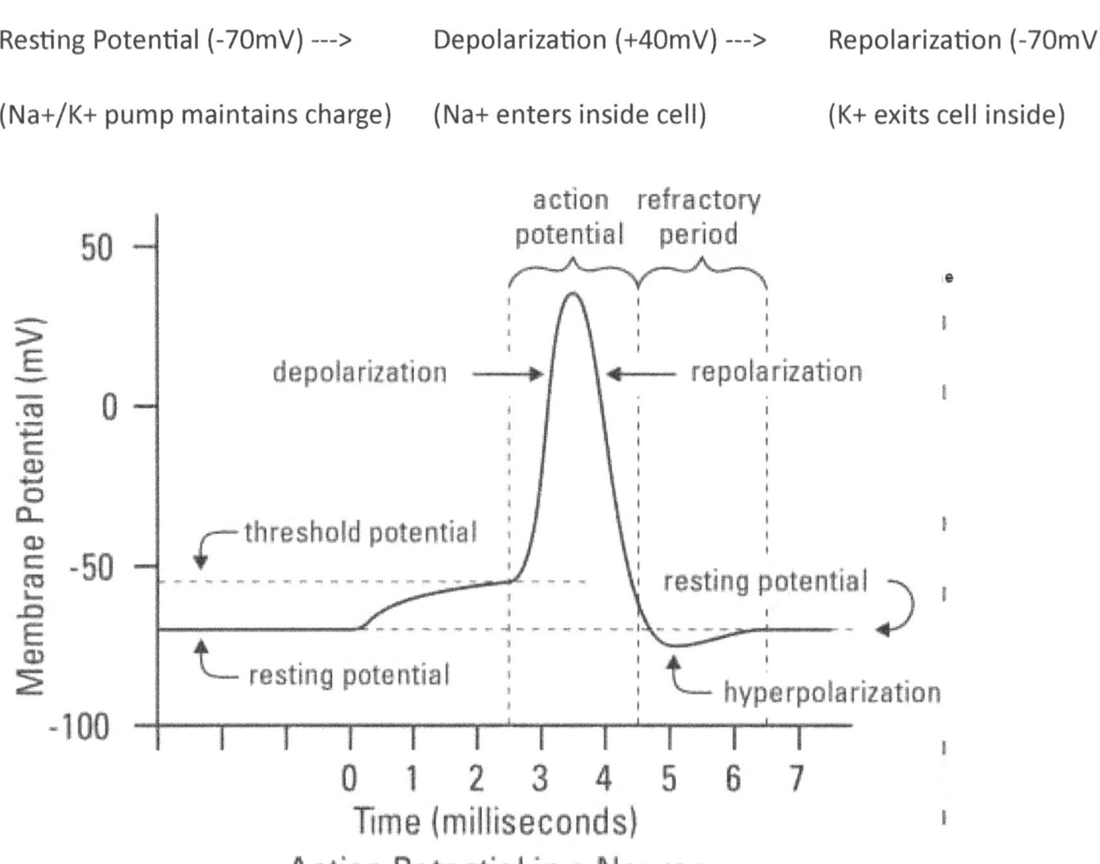

The electrical impulse that travels along the axon of a neuron is known as an **action potential**. This is a rapid change in electrical charge across the neuron's membrane, driven by ion movement.

Resting Membrane Potential (Before Excitation)

- Neurons are in a **resting state** when they are not transmitting an impulse.

- The inside of the neuron has a **negative charge (~ -70mV)** relative to the outside.

- This is maintained by the **sodium-potassium pump (Na+/K+ pump)**, which actively transports **3 Na+ ions out** and **2 K+ ions in**, keeping the inside more negative.

Generation of an Action Potential

When a neuron receives a strong enough stimulus, it undergoes several changes:

1. Depolarization (Excitation)

- If the stimulus reaches the **threshold potential (~ -55mV)**, voltage-gated **sodium (Na+) channels open**, allowing Na+ ions to rush inside.

- This causes the inside of the neuron to become **positive (~ +40mV)**.

- This rapid change in charge is called **depolarization**, leading to the firing of an action potential.

2. Propagation of the Action Potential

- The positive charge inside the neuron spreads along the axon.

- In **myelinated neurons**, the impulse jumps between the **Nodes of Ranvier** in a process called **saltatory conduction**, which speeds up transmission.

- In **unmyelinated neurons**, the impulse moves more slowly as it propagates continuously along the axon.

3. Repolarization (Restoration of Negative Charge)

- After depolarization, voltage-gated **potassium (K+) channels open**, allowing K+ ions to flow **out** of the neuron.

- This restores the **negative charge inside the neuron**.

4. Hyperpolarization and Refractory Period

- Sometimes, too much K+ leaves the cell, causing **hyperpolarization** (membrane potential drops below -70mV).

- During the **absolute refractory period**, another action potential **cannot** be generated, ensuring one-way conduction of the impulse.

- The **sodium-potassium pump** restores the resting potential, preparing the neuron for the next impulse.

2. Chemical Transmission: Synaptic Transmission

Once the action potential reaches the **axon terminals**, it triggers the release of neurotransmitters, which transmit the signal to the next neuron.

Electrical Signal > Ca^{2+} Influx > Neurotransmitter Release > Receptor Binding > Signal Transmission

Steps of Synaptic Transmission:

1. **Arrival of Action Potential**

o The electrical impulse reaches the axon terminals.

2. **Calcium Influx**

o Voltage-gated **calcium (Ca^{2+}) channels open**, allowing Ca^{2+} to enter the neuron.

3. **Neurotransmitter Release**

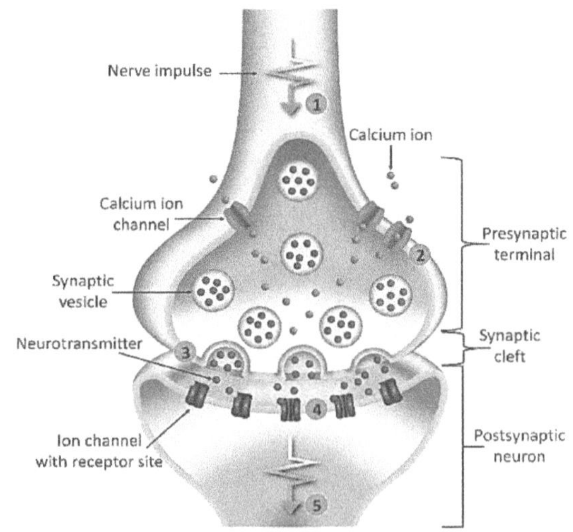

o The influx of Ca^{2+} causes vesicles filled with neurotransmitters (e.g., dopamine, serotonin) to fuse with the membrane and release their contents into the **synaptic cleft**.

4. **Binding to Receptors**

- Neurotransmitters bind to **receptors on the postsynaptic neuron**, triggering either:

  - **Excitatory Post-Synaptic Potential (EPSP):** Depolarizes the next neuron, making it more likely to fire.

  - **Inhibitory Post-Synaptic Potential (IPSP):** Hyperpolarizes the neuron, making it less likely to fire.

5. **Termination of Signal**

- The neurotransmitter is removed from the synaptic cleft by:

  - **Reuptake:** Neurotransmitters are reabsorbed by the presynaptic neuron (e.g., serotonin reuptake by SSRIs).

  - **Enzymatic Breakdown:** Enzymes degrade neurotransmitters (e.g., acetylcholinesterase breaks down acetylcholine).

  - **Diffusion:** Neurotransmitters drift away from the synapse.

Significance of Nerve Impulse Conduction in Physiological Psychology

- **Depression:** Low levels of serotonin due to excessive reuptake.

- **Schizophrenia:** Overactive dopamine transmission.

- **Epilepsy:** Uncontrolled electrical discharges in neurons.

- **Multiple Sclerosis (MS):** Damage to the myelin sheath slows or stops impulse conduction.

The conduction of a nerve impulse is a highly regulated process involving both **electrical** (action potential) and **chemical** (synaptic transmission) mechanisms. Disruptions in this process can lead to cognitive, emotional, and behavioural disorders, making it a crucial topic in physiological psychology.

NEUROMODULATORS

Neuromodulators are chemical messengers in the nervous system that regulate and modify the activity of neurons over a longer period, rather than directly triggering or inhibiting an immediate nerve impulse like neurotransmitters. Unlike neurotransmitters, which act quickly at specific synapses, neuromodulators diffuse over a larger area, affecting multiple neurons at once.

- **Neurotransmitters** → Act at specific synapses for fast communication.
- **Neuromodulators** → Spread over a wider area, altering neuron function over time.

Functions of Neuromodulators

Neuromodulators fine-tune the nervous system by:

✓ Regulating synaptic strength (making signals stronger or weaker).

✓ Modifying neural circuits (affecting multiple neurons at once).

✓ Enhancing or suppressing neurotransmitter release.

✓ Influencing emotions, learning, attention, and pain perception.

Neuromodulators affect neurons by:

1. **Altering neurotransmitter release** (e.g., serotonin enhances mood by increasing synaptic activity).

2. **Changing receptor sensitivity** (e.g., dopamine can make neurons more responsive to stimulation).

3. **Modifying gene expression** (long-term brain plasticity changes).

Neuromodulators play a **crucial role in shaping neural communication** by modulating neurotransmitter activity over time. They are vital for **learning, memory, mood, attention, pain perception, and movement**. Their dysfunction is linked to **neurological and psychiatric disorders**, making them key targets for treatments like **SSRIs, L-Dopa, and antipsychotic drugs**.

NERVOUS SYSTEMS

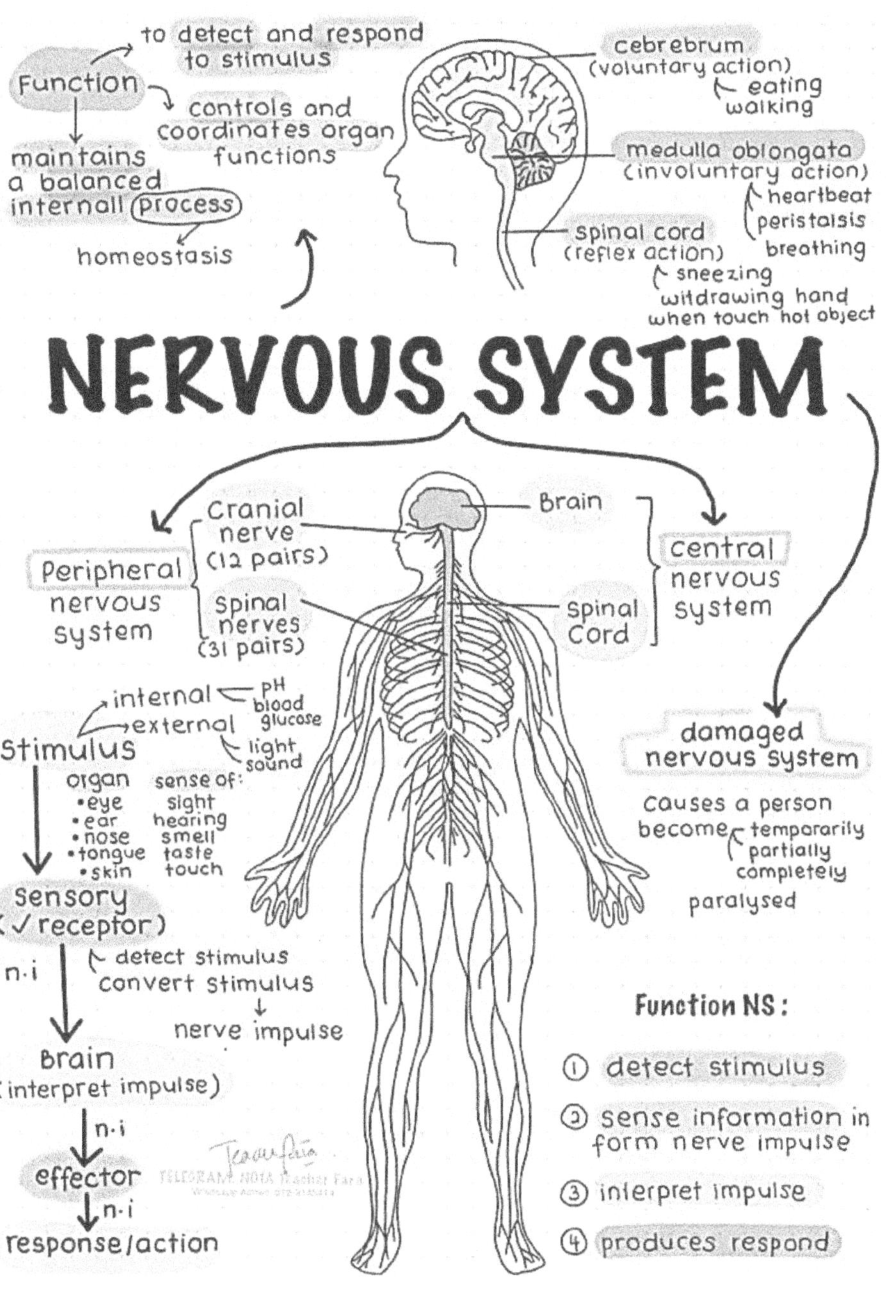

Central Nervous System (CNS)

The **Central Nervous System (CNS)** consists of the **brain and spinal cord**. It is responsible for **processing, interpreting, and responding to sensory information**.

Features of the CNS:

- Acts as the **command center** of the body.

- Controls **thoughts, emotions, and behaviours**.

- Integrates **sensory input and motor output**.

- Protected by the **skull, vertebrae, meninges, and cerebrospinal fluid (CSF)**.

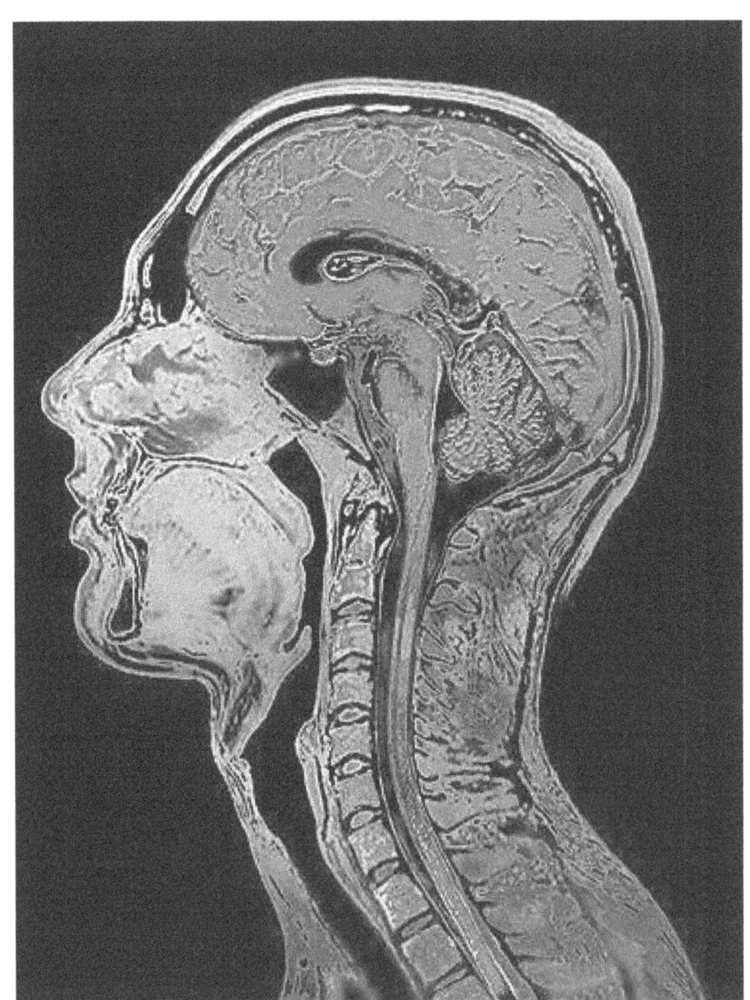

Components of the CNS:

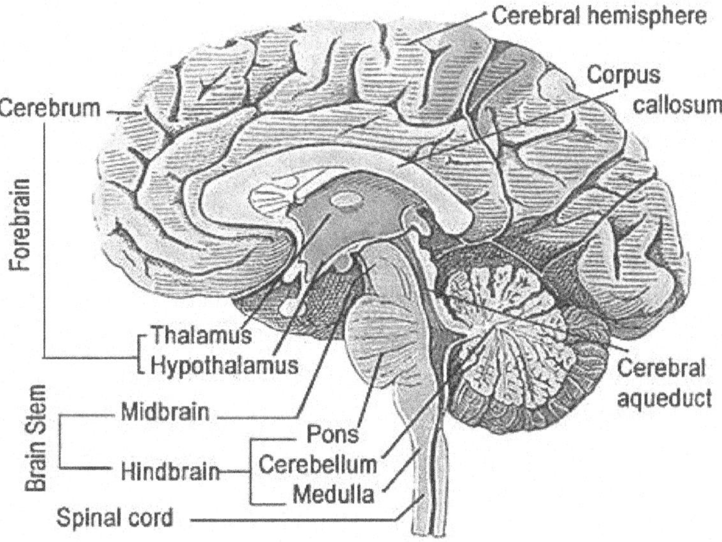

1. **Brain**

Includes structures like the **cerebral cortex, limbic system, thalamus, hypothalamus, cerebellum, and brainstem**.

- o   Controls **higher cognitive functions (thinking, memory, problem-solving)**.

- o   Regulates **autonomic functions** (breathing, heart rate).

2. **Spinal Cord**:

- o   Acts as a **communication highway** between the brain and the body.

- o   Controls **reflexes and motor responses**.

Figure 1 Structure of Brain

2. Peripheral Nervous System (PNS)

The **Peripheral Nervous System (PNS)** consists of all the **nerves and ganglia outside the brain and spinal cord**. It connects the **CNS to the limbs and organs**.

Features of the PNS:

- Transmits **sensory and motor signals** between the CNS and the body.

- Controls **voluntary and involuntary functions**.

- Divided into two main parts:

    1. **Somatic Nervous System (SNS)**: Controls **voluntary movements** (skeletal muscles).

    2. **Autonomic Nervous System (ANS)**: Controls **involuntary functions** (heartbeat, digestion).

    - Further divided into:

    - **Sympathetic Nervous System** ("Fight or Flight" response).

    - **Parasympathetic Nervous System** ("Rest and Digest" response).

3. Difference Between CNS and PNS

Feature	Central Nervous System (CNS)	Peripheral Nervous System (PNS)
Location	Brain and spinal cord	Nerves and ganglia outside CNS
Function	Processes and interprets sensory data, controls motor responses	Transmits sensory and motor signals between CNS and body
Protection	Protected by skull, vertebrae, meninges, and cerebrospinal fluid (CSF)	Not protected by bones or CSF, making it more vulnerable to injury
Control	Responsible for **higher-order functions** like thinking, memory, emotions, and movement control	Responsible for **sending commands** to organs, muscles, and glands
Components	Brain (forebrain, midbrain, hindbrain) and spinal cord	Somatic Nervous System (SNS) and Autonomic Nervous System (ANS)
Disorders	Stroke, epilepsy, multiple sclerosis, Alzheimer's disease	Neuropathy, Guillain-Barré syndrome, autonomic dysfunction

4. How CNS and PNS Work Together

- The **CNS** processes sensory information received from the **PNS**.

- The **CNS** then sends motor commands back to the **PNS**, which **controls movement and organ function**.

- Example:

    o If you touch a hot stove, **PNS sensory neurons** send pain signals to the **CNS**.

    o The **CNS processes this information** and sends a command via **PNS motor neurons** to move your hand away.

The **Central Nervous System (CNS)**—comprising the **brain and spinal cord**—plays a crucial role in controlling bodily functions and behaviour. The CNS is responsible for **sensory processing, motor control, and cognition**, ensuring coordinated interaction between external stimuli and internal responses.

1. Sensory Processing in the CNS

Sensory processing involves the reception, transmission, and interpretation of stimuli from the **external** and **internal** environments. The CNS, particularly the **brain**, is responsible for processing different sensory modalities, including vision, hearing, touch, taste, and smell.

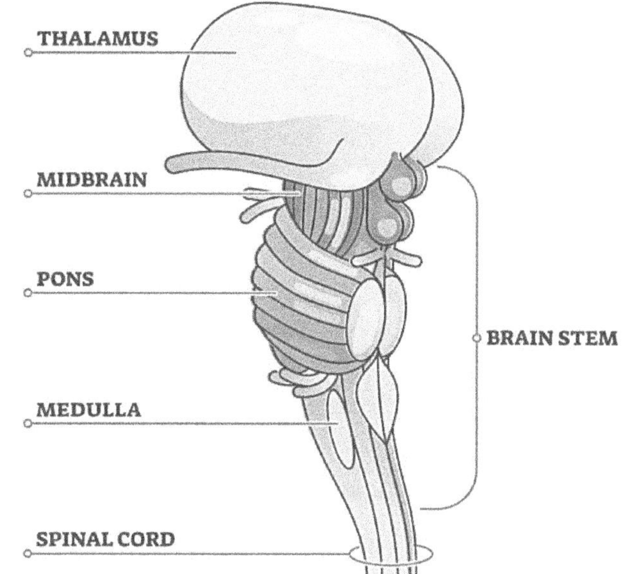

Figure 2 Brain Stem

Pathway of Sensory Processing

1. **Sensory Receptors:** Detect environmental stimuli (e.g., light, sound, pressure).

2. **Peripheral Nervous System (PNS):** Transmits sensory signals via **afferent neurons** to the spinal cord.

3. **Spinal Cord:** Relays sensory information to the **brainstem and thalamus**.

4. **Thalamus:** Acts as a relay station, sending signals to the appropriate **cortical regions**.

5. **Primary Sensory Cortices:** Specialized areas in the **cerebral cortex** process specific sensory modalities.

CNS Structures Involved in Sensory Processing

- **Thalamus:** Routes sensory signals (except smell) to the cerebral cortex.

- **Primary Sensory Cortices:**

  - **Visual Cortex (Occipital Lobe):** Processes visual information.

  - **Auditory Cortex (Temporal Lobe):** Processes sound perception.

  - **Somatosensory Cortex (Parietal Lobe):** Detects touch, pain, temperature, and proprioception.

  - **Olfactory Bulb (Frontal Lobe):** Processes smell directly without thalamic relay.

Example Damage to the **primary visual cortex** can lead to **cortical blindness**, even if the eyes and optic nerves function normally.

- A stroke affecting the **somatosensory cortex** can cause **loss of sensation** on the opposite side of the body.

2. Motor Control in the CNS

Motor control involves the planning, initiation, and execution of voluntary and involuntary movements. The **CNS controls motor functions** through interactions between the **cerebral cortex, basal ganglia, cerebellum, brainstem, and spinal cord**.

Pathway of Motor Control

1. **Motor Planning (Frontal Cortex):** Initiates voluntary movement.

2. **Basal Ganglia & Cerebellum:** Modulate and refine movement.

3. **Motor Cortex (Precentral Gyrus):** Sends motor commands.

4. **Brainstem & Spinal Cord:** Relay signals to peripheral nerves.

5. **Skeletal Muscles:** Execute the movement.

CNS Structures Involved in Motor Control

- **Primary Motor Cortex (M1):** Directs voluntary movements by sending signals to muscles via the **corticospinal tract**.

- **Basal Ganglia:** Plays a role in movement initiation and coordination (affected in **Parkinson's disease**).

- **Cerebellum:** Fine-tunes movement, maintaining balance and coordination.

- **Brainstem:** Regulates involuntary movements like posture and breathing.

Example

- **Lesions in the cerebellum** lead to **ataxia**, a condition characterized by lack of coordination.

- **Parkinson's disease** results from basal ganglia dysfunction, leading to **tremors and slowed movement (bradykinesia)**.

3. Cognition and the CNS

Cognition refers to higher-order brain functions, including **thinking, reasoning, problem-solving, learning, memory, language, and decision-making**. These functions are primarily controlled by the **cerebral cortex**, particularly the **prefrontal cortex** and **association areas**.

Cognitive Processes Controlled by the CNS

1. **Memory & Learning:**

   o **Hippocampus (Temporal Lobe):** Essential for encoding new memories.

   o **Prefrontal Cortex:** Involved in working memory and decision-making.

2. **Attention & Perception:**

   o **Parietal Lobe:** Directs attention to important stimuli.

- o **Temporal Lobe:** Processes auditory and visual perception.

3. **Language Processing:**

- o **Broca's Area (Frontal Lobe):** Speech production.

- o **Wernicke's Area (Temporal Lobe):** Language comprehension.

4. **Emotion & Decision-Making:**

- o **Amygdala:** Regulates emotional responses (e.g., fear, aggression).

- o **Prefrontal Cortex:** Helps in rational decision-making and impulse control.

Example

- **Damage to the hippocampus** results in **anterograde amnesia** (inability to form new memories).

- **Lesions in Broca's area** cause **Broca's aphasia**, leading to difficulty in speech production while comprehension remains intact.

CNS Roles in Behaviour

Function	CNS Structures Involved	Disorders if Damaged
Sensory Processing	Thalamus, Sensory Cortex, Brainstem	Cortical blindness, sensory loss
Motor Control	Motor Cortex, Basal Ganglia, Cerebellum	Parkinson's, Ataxia, Paralysis
Cognition	Prefrontal Cortex, Hippocampus, Amygdala	Amnesia, Aphasia, Impulsivity

Major Divisions of the Central Nervous System (CNS)

The **Central Nervous System (CNS)** consists of the **brain and spinal cord**, responsible for processing sensory information, coordinating movement, regulating emotions, and higher cognitive functions.

The **brain** is divided into **three major regions**:

Figure 3 Major divisions of Brain

1. **Forebrain (Prosencephalon)** – Higher cognitive functions, emotions, and sensory processing.

2. **Midbrain (Mesencephalon)** – Relay center for sensory and motor pathways.

3. **Hindbrain (Rhombencephalon)** – Controls basic survival functions, movement, and coordination.

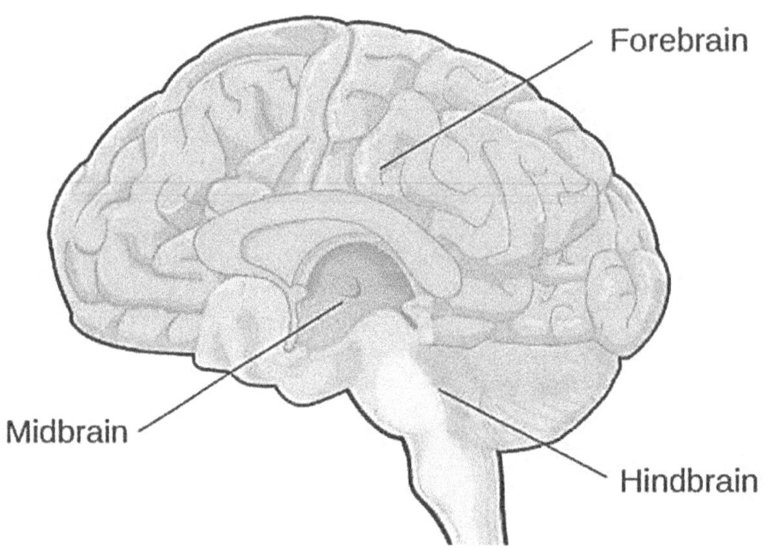

The Brain: Structural and Functional Organization

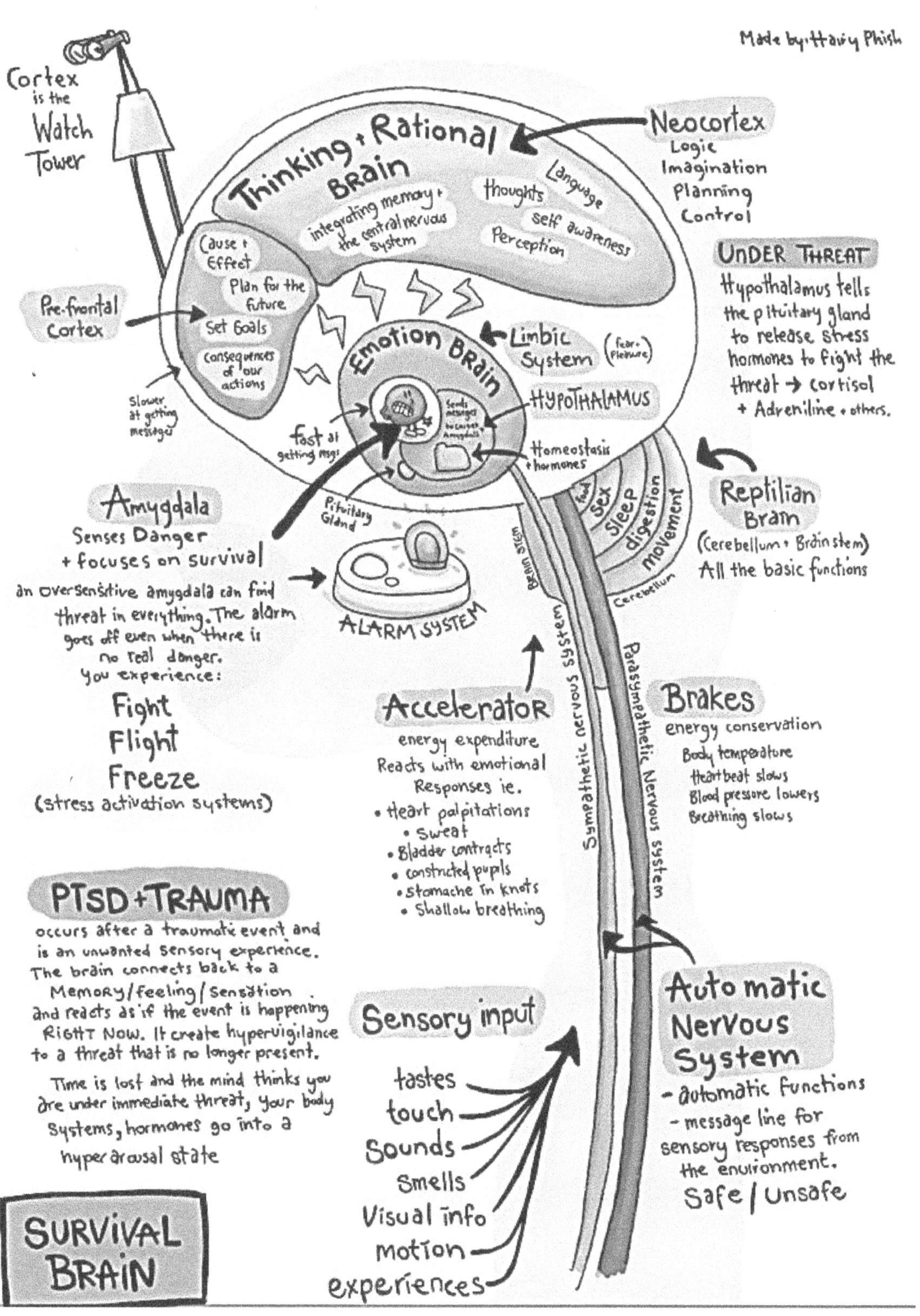

FOREBRAIN STRUCTURES

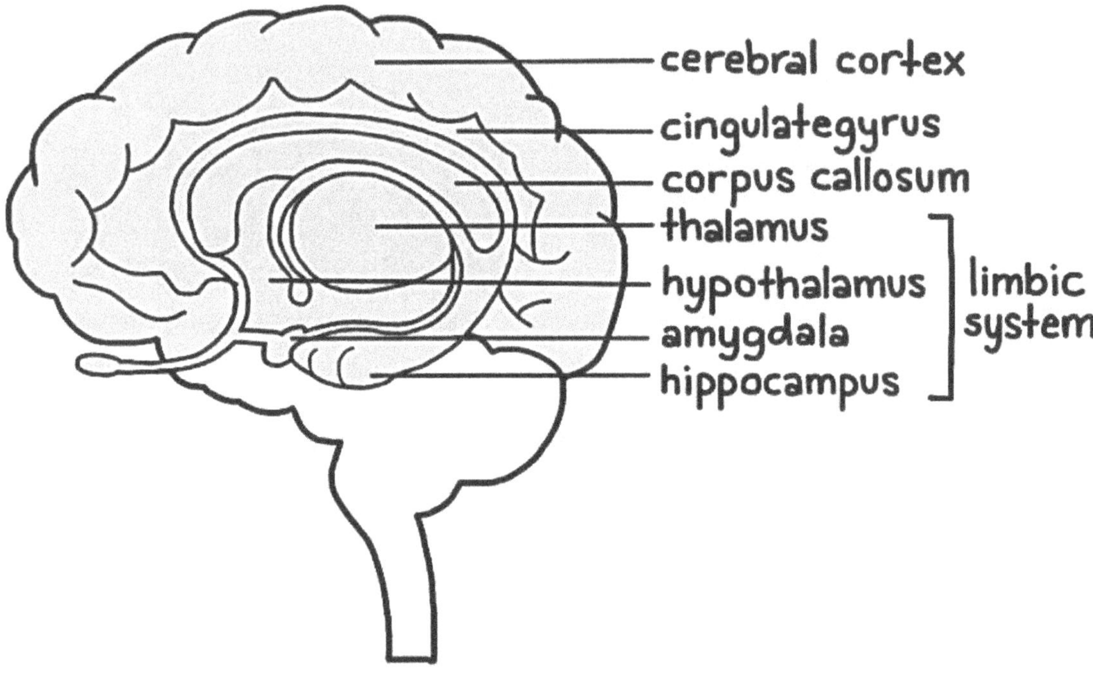

<u>Forebrain (Prosencephalon)</u>

Figure 4 Forebrain and its parts

The forebrain is the most evolved and largest part of the human brain. It is involved in higher cognitive functions, emotions, sensory processing, voluntary movements, and homeostasis. It consists of two primary subdivisions:

1. **Telencephalon** (includes the Cerebral Cortex, Basal Ganglia, and Limbic System)

2. **Diencephalon** (includes the Thalamus and Hypothalamus)

1. Cerebral Cortex: Lobes of the Brain and Their Functions

The cerebral cortex is the outermost layer of the brain and is responsible for higher-order cognitive functions, including perception, decision-making, voluntary movements, and language.

It is divided into four major lobes:

Parts of the Human Brain

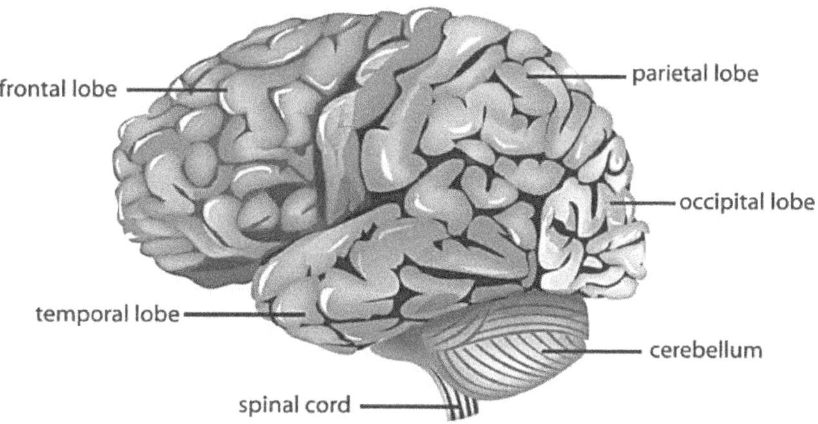

Figure 5 Lobes of Brain

A. Frontal Lobe (*Executive Control & Motor Function*)

- Located at the front of the brain.

- Responsible for executive functions such as planning, problem-solving, impulse control, social behaviour, and voluntary movement.

- Contains the Primary Motor Cortex (Precentral Gyrus): Controls voluntary muscle movements.

- Prefrontal Cortex: Critical for personality, decision-making, and social interactions.

- *Broca's Area* (Left Hemisphere): Responsible for speech production (damage leads to Broca's aphasia, difficulty in speech production).

- *Example of Dysfunction*: Damage to the frontal lobe can cause personality changes, impulsivity, or impaired judgment (as seen in Phineas Gage's case).

B. Parietal Lobe (*Sensory Processing & Spatial Awareness*)

- Located behind the frontal lobe.

- Contains the Primary Somatosensory Cortex (Postcentral Gyrus), responsible for processing touch, temperature, and pain sensations.

- Plays a role in spatial awareness and navigation.

- Involved in mathematical reasoning and understanding numbers.

- Example of Dysfunction: Damage to the right parietal lobe can cause hemispatial neglect syndrome (inability to perceive stimuli on one side of space).

C. Temporal Lobe (*Hearing, Memory & Language Comprehension*)

- Located on the sides of the brain.

- Contains the Primary Auditory Cortex, responsible for processing sounds.

- Includes Wernicke's Area (Left Hemisphere), responsible for language comprehension (damage causes Wernicke's aphasia, where a person can speak fluently but makes no sense).

- Plays a significant role in memory formation due to its connection with the hippocampus.

- Example of Dysfunction: Damage to the temporal lobe can result in memory loss, language difficulties, or auditory hallucinations (as seen in schizophrenia).

D. Occipital Lobe (*Vision & Visual Processing*)

- Located at the back of the brain.

- Contains the Primary Visual Cortex (V1), responsible for processing visual information.

- Damage can lead to cortical blindness or visual agnosia (inability to recognize objects visually).

- Example of Dysfunction: Lesions in the occipital lobe can lead to visual hallucinations or loss of specific aspects of vision (e.g., color blindness, motion blindness).

2. Basal Ganglia: Role in Movement and Disorders (e.g., Parkinson's Disease)

The Basal Ganglia is a collection of subcortical nuclei involved in movement regulation, habit formation, motivation, and reward processing.

Structure of the Basal Ganglia

The three primary components include:

1. **Caudate Nucleus**

2. **Putamen**

3. **Globus Pallidus**

Function of the Basal Ganglia

- Initiates and modulates voluntary movements.

- Plays a role in motor learning, reward-based learning, and habit formation.

Disorders Related to Basal Ganglia Dysfunction

1. *Parkinson's Disease* (*Hypokinetic Disorder*)

- Caused by dopamine depletion in the substantia nigra.

- Leads to tremors, bradykinesia (slowness of movement), muscle rigidity, and postural instability.

2. *Huntington's Disease* (*Hyperkinetic Disorder*)

- A genetic disorder that causes progressive neuronal degeneration in the caudate nucleus.

- Leads to involuntary movements (chorea), cognitive decline, and psychiatric symptoms.

4. Limbic System: Emotions & Memory (Hippocampus, Amygdala)

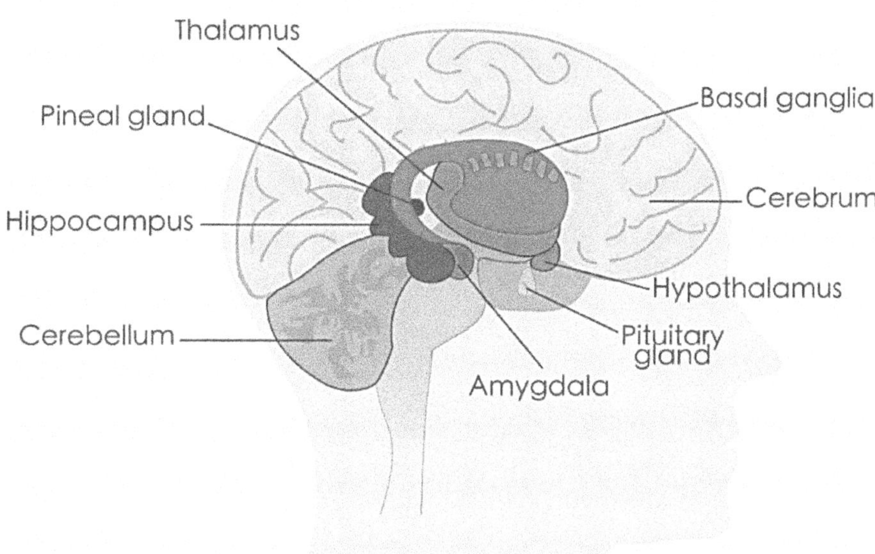

Figure 7: Limbic system

The Limbic System is involved in emotion, memory processing, motivation, and behaviour.

A. Hippocampus (*Memory Formation & Learning*)

- Essential for converting short-term memory into long-term memory.

- Plays a role in spatial navigation.

- Damage leads to anterograde amnesia (inability to form new memories), as seen in the case of patient H.M.

B. Amygdala (*Emotional Processing & Fear Response*)

- Crucial for processing emotions such as fear, aggression, and pleasure.

- Involved in threat detection and fight-or-flight responses.

- Overactivity is linked to anxiety disorders, PTSD, and phobias.

4. Thalamus & Hypothalamus: Sensory Relay & Homeostasis

A. Thalamus (Sensory Relay Station)

- Receives sensory input from the body and relays it to the cerebral cortex.

- Processes information related to vision, hearing, touch, and taste (but NOT smell).

- Plays a role in consciousness, attention, and sleep-wake cycles.

- Damage can lead to sensory deficits or thalamic pain syndrome.

B. Hypothalamus (Homeostasis & Endocrine Control)

- Regulates body temperature, hunger, thirst, sleep, and circadian rhythms.

- Controls the autonomic nervous system (ANS) and endocrine system via the pituitary gland.

- Governs hormonal regulation, including stress hormones (cortisol).

- Involved in sexual behaviour, aggression, and motivation.

- Example of Dysfunction:

  - Hypothalamic Lesions → Can cause disruptions in body temperature, eating disorders (hyperphagia or anorexia), and hormonal imbalances.

2. Midbrain (Mesencephalon)

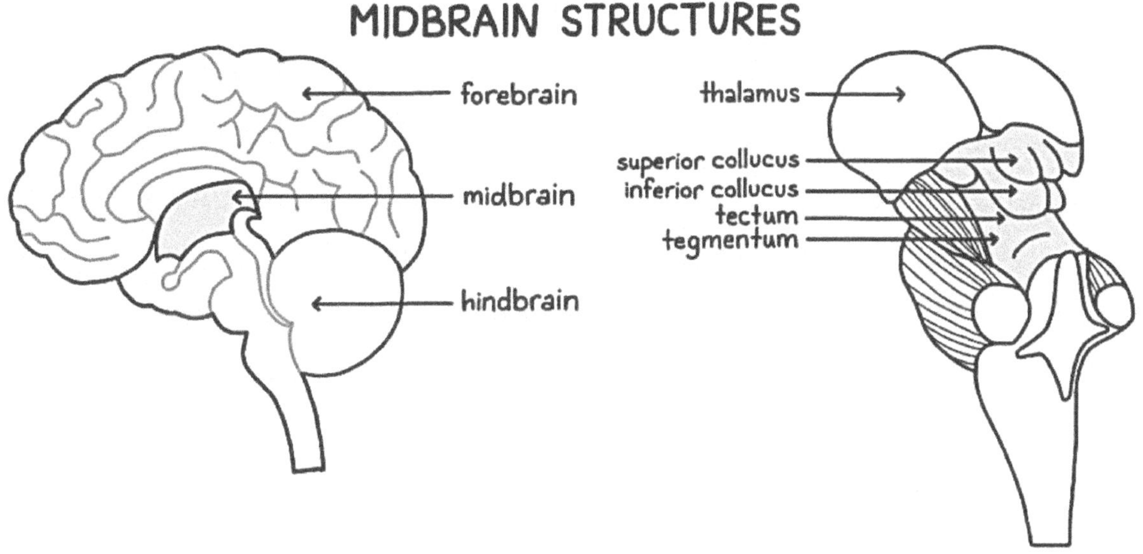

Figure 8 Midbrain and its parts

The **midbrain (mesencephalon)** is a critical structure in the central nervous system (CNS) that serves as a **bridge between the forebrain and hindbrain**. It plays an essential role in **sensory processing, motor control, and reflexive responses to stimuli**. Two of its most significant structures are the **tectum and tegmentum**, which are involved in **visual and auditory processing, movement regulation, and alertness**.

1. Tectum (Latin for "Roof")

The **tectum** is the **dorsal (top) part of the midbrain** and is primarily responsible for **processing sensory information and controlling reflexive movements related to vision and hearing**. It contains two important structures:

A. Superior Colliculus – Visual Processing & Reflexes

The **superior colliculus** is involved in **visual attention, tracking, and eye movements**.

- **Visual Orientation:** It helps direct gaze movements toward objects of interest.

- **Saccadic Eye Movements:** Rapid eye movements that help scan the environment for important visual stimuli.

- **Reflexive Eye and Head Movements:** It mediates reflexes like turning the head toward a sudden movement in the periphery.

- **Integration with Other Sensory Modalities:** It works with the **inferior colliculus** and **somatosensory system** to coordinate responses to stimuli.

◇ **Example**: If you hear a loud noise and automatically turn your head toward the sound, your **superior colliculus** is responsible for this rapid, reflexive action.

B. Inferior Colliculus – Auditory Processing & Reflexes

The **inferior colliculus** is involved in **auditory signal processing and sound localization**.

- **Receives Auditory Inputs from the Brainstem:** It integrates signals from the **cochlear nuclei** and **superior olivary complex**.

- **Sound Localization:** Helps determine the **direction and distance of sounds** in the environment.

- **Startle Reflex:** Plays a role in **automatic reactions** to sudden loud noises.

- **Integration with the Superior Colliculus:** Helps coordinate auditory and visual reflexes for better orientation to stimuli.

◇ **Example**: If someone suddenly claps their hands behind you, the **inferior colliculus** helps identify the location of the sound and triggers a **startle response**.

2. Tegmentum (Latin for "Covering")

The **tegmentum** is the **ventral (bottom) part of the midbrain**, containing important structures involved in **motor control, arousal, pain modulation, and autonomic regulation**.

A. Periaqueductal Gray (PAG) – Pain Modulation & Defensive Behaviour

- **Regulates Pain Perception:** The PAG is involved in **opioid-mediated pain suppression** (endogenous analgesia).

- **Endorphin Release:** It plays a role in reducing pain sensitivity through the release of **endorphins**.

- **Defense Mechanisms:** Triggers **fight-or-flight responses** in threatening situations.

◇ **Example**: If you get injured but don't feel pain immediately due to an adrenaline rush, the **PAG** is responsible for suppressing pain signals.

B. Red Nucleus – Motor Coordination & Muscle Tone

- **Controls Movement of the Limbs:** The red nucleus is involved in **fine motor coordination**, especially **arm and hand movements**.

- **Part of the Extrapyramidal Motor System:** Works with the **cerebellum** and **spinal cord** for smooth motor function.

◇ **Example**: If a cat's **red nucleus** is damaged, it will struggle with **coordinated paw movements** when reaching for objects.

C. Substantia Nigra – Dopamine Production & Motor Control

- **Produces Dopamine:** The **substantia nigra pars compacta** (SNc) is a major producer of **dopamine**, a neurotransmitter crucial for **voluntary movement**.

- **Parkinson's Disease Connection:** Degeneration of dopamine neurons in the substantia nigra leads to **tremors, rigidity, and bradykinesia** (slowed movement).

- **Part of the Basal Ganglia Circuit:** The substantia nigra communicates with the **striatum** (caudate nucleus & putamen) to regulate **motor function and reward processing**.

◇ **Example**: In Parkinson's disease, the loss of **dopaminergic neurons** in the **substantia nigra** leads to **difficulty initiating movements** and **tremors at rest**.

D. Reticular Formation – Arousal, Attention & Sleep-Wake Cycle

- **Regulates Arousal & Consciousness:** The **reticular activating system (RAS)** controls alertness and attention.

- **Influences Sleep-Wake Cycles:** Helps regulate the **transition between sleep and wakefulness**.

- **Autonomic Functions:** Plays a role in heart rate, respiration, and reflex control.

◇ **Example :** Damage to the **reticular formation** can lead to **coma or severe drowsiness** due to impaired arousal mechanisms.

Functions of the Midbrain's Tectum & Tegmentum

Midbrain Structure	Primary Function	Example of Function
Tectum	Controls reflexive movements in response to visual and auditory stimuli	Turning head toward a sudden loud sound
Superior Colliculus	Visual reflexes, eye movements, tracking	Automatic eye movement following a moving object
Inferior Colliculus	Auditory processing, sound localization	Startle response to unexpected noise
Tegmentum	Motor control, pain regulation, arousal	Coordinating arm movements, suppressing pain
Periaqueductal Gray (PAG)	Pain modulation, fight-or-flight response	Decreased pain perception in stressful situations
Red Nucleus	Motor coordination of limbs	Controlling precise hand movements
Substantia Nigra	Dopamine production, voluntary movement	Degeneration leads to Parkinson's disease

Reticular Formation	Arousal, attention, sleep-wake cycle	Regulating alertness and sleep patterns

The **midbrain (mesencephalon)** plays a vital role in **processing sensory information, controlling reflexive movements, regulating motor coordination, and maintaining consciousness**. The **tectum** is primarily responsible for **visual and auditory reflexes**, while the **tegmentum** contributes to **movement regulation, pain suppression, and arousal mechanisms**. Understanding the **functional integration** of these structures helps explain many **neurological and psychological conditions**, including **Parkinson's disease, attention disorders, and pain perception abnormalities**.

3. Hindbrain (Rhombencephalon)

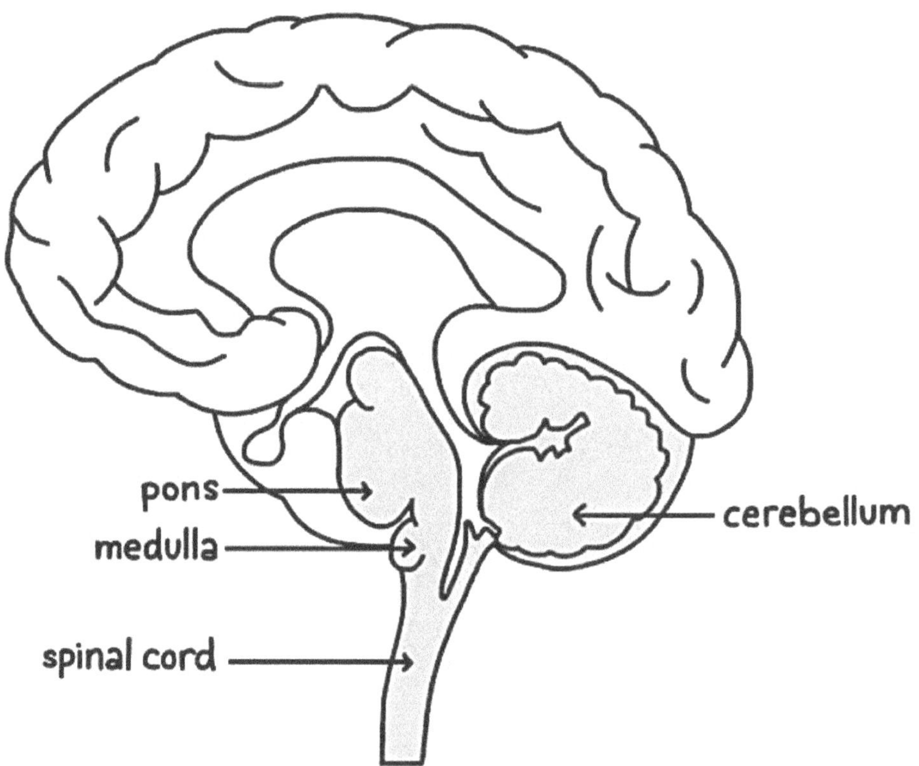

Figure 9 Hindbrain and its parts

The **hindbrain (rhombencephalon)** is the most **posterior (lower) region** of the brain and is crucial for **basic survival functions**, including movement coordination, balance, autonomic regulation (such as breathing and heart rate), and reflexive responses. It consists of three major structures:

1. **Cerebellum** (Coordination and Balance)

2. **Pons** (Bridge between brain regions; autonomic and sensory functions)

3. **Medulla Oblongata** (Vital autonomic control center)

1. Cerebellum: Coordination and Balance

Structure of the Cerebellum

- The **cerebellum** is located at the **posterior base of the brain**, just above the brainstem and behind the pons.

- It has a highly folded surface (like the cerebral cortex), increasing surface area for neural connections.

- Composed of **two hemispheres** separated by the **vermis (a central region)**.

- Internally, it consists of:

  - **Cerebellar cortex** (outer layer of gray matter)
  - **Deep cerebellar nuclei** (clusters of neurons that relay signals)
  - **White matter tracts** (for communication with the rest of the brain)

Function of the Cerebellum

The cerebellum is primarily involved in:

1. **Coordination of movement**

   - It **receives input from the motor cortex, sensory systems, and spinal cord**.
   - Ensures **smooth, precise, and coordinated voluntary movements**.
   - Controls **timing, force, and accuracy of muscle actions**.

2. **Balance and Posture Regulation**

   - Uses **vestibular information from the inner ear** to help maintain balance.
   - Helps adjust posture when standing, walking, or engaging in movement.

3. **Motor Learning & Adaptation**

   - Plays a role in **learning new motor skills** (e.g., riding a bike, playing an instrument).
   - Uses **error correction**—if a movement is incorrect, the cerebellum adjusts it.

4. **Cognitive and Emotional Processing** (Lesser-Known Functions)

- o   Recent research suggests the cerebellum may also be involved in **cognition, attention, and emotion regulation**.

Damage to the Cerebellum: Effects & Disorders

- **Ataxia**: Loss of coordinated movements (e.g., clumsy walking, difficulty grasping objects).

- **Dysmetria**: Inability to judge distances accurately (e.g., overshooting or undershooting when reaching for something).

- **Intention Tremor**: Trembling movements that occur when performing voluntary tasks.

- **Vestibular Dysfunction**: Issues with balance, dizziness, and vertigo.

2. Pons: The Brain's Communication Bridge

Structure of the Pons

- The **pons** is located above the **medulla oblongata** and below the **midbrain**.

- It is **bulbous in shape** and acts as a **relay center** between different parts of the brain.

- It contains:

  - o   **Cranial nerve nuclei** (involved in facial sensations and motor control)

  - o   **White matter tracts** that connect the cerebellum to the rest of the brain

  - o   **Pontine reticular formation** (involved in sleep and arousal)

Functions of the Pons

1. **Relay Station Between Brain and Cerebellum**

   - o   Transmits motor signals from the **cerebral cortex to the cerebellum** for movement coordination.

2. **Regulation of Sleep and Arousal**

   - o   Works closely with the **reticular activating system (RAS)** to regulate sleep-wake cycles.

   - o   Plays a role in **REM sleep and dreaming**.

3. **Control of Facial Movements and Sensations**

   - o   Houses nuclei for **cranial nerves** controlling facial expressions, chewing, and eye movements.

4. **Autonomic Functions**

   - o   Helps regulate **respiration rate** along with the medulla.

Damage to the Pons: Effects & Disorders

- **Locked-in Syndrome**: A condition where an individual is conscious but unable to move or speak, except for blinking.

- **Respiratory Dysfunction**: Can lead to irregular breathing patterns.

- **Loss of Facial Sensation or Movement**: Due to cranial nerve involvement.

3. Medulla Oblongata: The Vital Autonomic Center

Structure of the Medulla Oblongata

- The **medulla oblongata** is located at the **base of the brainstem**, just above the spinal cord.

- It contains several **cranial nerve nuclei** and **white matter pathways** that connect the brain to the spinal cord.

- Internally, it consists of:

  - **Pyramidal tracts** (descending motor signals from the brain to the body).

  - **Olives (inferior olivary nuclei)** that coordinate motor control.

  - **Vital autonomic centers** controlling life-sustaining functions.

Functions of the Medulla Oblongata

1. **Autonomic Control of Vital Functions**

   - **Heart Rate & Blood Pressure Regulation** (via the cardiac center)

   - **Breathing Control** (via the respiratory center)

   - **Reflexive Actions** like sneezing, coughing, swallowing, and vomiting

2. **Motor & Sensory Pathways**

   - Acts as a **relay station** for sensory and motor pathways traveling between the brain and spinal cord.

3. **Cranial Nerve Function**

   - Controls **swallowing, tongue movement, and gag reflex**.

4. **Regulation of Consciousness and Alertness**

   - Works with the **reticular formation** to regulate alertness and wakefulness.

Damage to the Medulla Oblongata: Effects & Disorders

- **Respiratory Failure**: Can be fatal if breathing control is lost.

- **Cardiac Arrest or Blood Pressure Dysregulation**: Due to the loss of autonomic function.

- **Loss of Reflexes**: Difficulty swallowing, coughing, and regulating balance.

Brain Divisions and Functions

Brain Division	Subdivisions	Key Functions
Forebrain (Prosencephalon)	**Telencephalon** – Cerebral Cortex, Basal Ganglia, Limbic System **Diencephalon** – Thalamus, Hypothalamus	Higher cognition, emotions, sensory processing, movement regulation, endocrine control
Midbrain (Mesencephalon)	Tectum (Superior & Inferior Colliculi) Tegmentum (PAG, Red Nucleus, Substantia Nigra)	Sensory-motor integration, reflexes, reward processing
Hindbrain (Rhombencephalon)	**Metencephalon** – Cerebellum, Pons **Myelencephalon** – Medulla Oblongata	Balance, coordination, autonomic functions (breathing, heart rate)

Spinal Cord: Structure & Function

The **spinal cord** is a vital part of the **Central Nervous System (CNS)**, responsible for transmitting **sensory (afferent) information** from the body to the brain and sending **motor (efferent) commands** from the brain to the muscles. It also plays a crucial role in **reflex actions** and contains circuits that allow for **automatic responses** to stimuli.

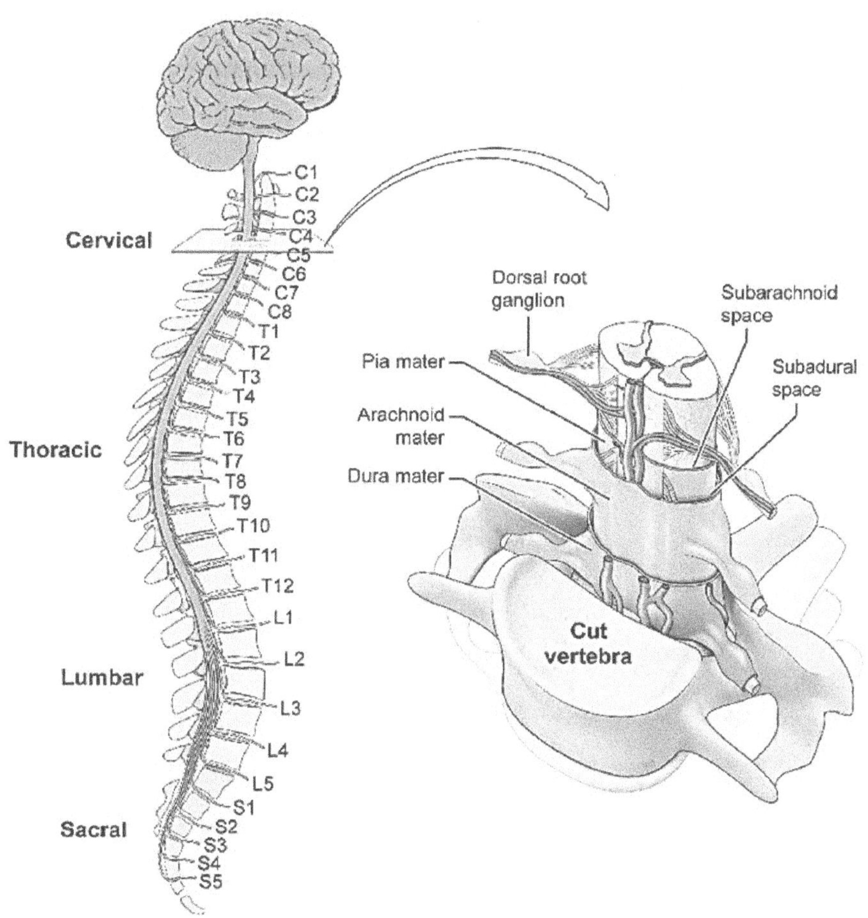

Figure 10 Spinal Cord

Structure of the Spinal Cord

1.1 General Anatomy

The spinal cord is a **long, cylindrical structure** extending from the **medulla oblongata** of the brainstem down to the lower back. It is housed within the **vertebral column**, which protects it.

- Divided into **four main regions**:
  - **Cervical (C1-C8)** – Controls the neck, shoulders, arms, and hands
  - **Thoracic (T1-T12)** – Controls the upper back and abdomen
  - **Lumbar (L1-L5)** – Controls the lower back and legs
  - **Sacral (S1-S5)** – Controls the pelvis, bladder, and feet
- The **spinal nerves** exit the spinal cord through spaces between the vertebrae, forming part of the **Peripheral Nervous System (PNS)**.
- The **cauda equina ("horse's tail")** is a bundle of nerve roots at the lower end of the spinal cord, responsible for **lower limb and pelvic organ function**.

1.2 Internal Structure

The spinal cord is composed of **gray matter and white matter**:

- **Gray Matter (Inner Region)** – Contains **neuronal cell bodies** and is shaped like a butterfly.
  - **Dorsal horn (posterior):** Processes **sensory (afferent) input** from the body.
  - **Ventral horn (anterior):** Contains **motor neurons** that send commands to muscles.
- **White Matter (Outer Region)** – Composed of **myelinated axons** that form **ascending (sensory) and descending (motor) pathways** connecting the spinal cord to the brain.

2. Ascending (Sensory) and Descending (Motor) Pathways

The spinal cord contains **tracts** that carry signals **to and from** the brain. These are divided into:

2.1 Ascending (Sensory) Pathways – Carry sensory information (touch, pain, temperature, proprioception) from the body to the brain.

There are three major ascending pathways:

1. Dorsal Column-Medial Lemniscus Pathway (DCML)

- **Function:** Carries fine **touch, vibration, and proprioception** (body position).

- **Pathway:**
  - Sensory neurons enter through the **dorsal root ganglion**.
  - Signals travel up the **dorsal columns** (gracile and cuneate fasciculus).
  - Synapse in the **medulla**, where they cross to the opposite side.
  - Continue to the **thalamus** and then to the **somatosensory cortex**.

2. Spinothalamic Tract (Anterolateral System)

- **Function:** Transmits **pain, temperature, and crude touch**.
- **Pathway:**
  - Sensory neurons synapse in the **spinal cord** (dorsal horn).
  - Axons cross immediately to the opposite side.
  - Travel up the **spinal cord to the thalamus**.
  - Relayed to the **somatosensory cortex**.

3. Spinocerebellar Tract

- **Function:** Sends **proprioceptive information** (body position) to the **cerebellum** for coordination.
- **Pathway:**
  - Signals from muscles and joints travel up the **spinal cord**.
  - Some fibers cross, while others remain on the same side.
  - Information is sent to the **cerebellum** to fine-tune movement.

2.2 Descending (Motor) Pathways – Carry motor commands from the brain to muscles.

Two major descending pathways control voluntary and involuntary movement:

1. Corticospinal Tract (Pyramidal Tract)

- **Function:** Controls **voluntary muscle movements**.
- **Pathway:**
  - Originates in the **motor cortex**.
  - Crosses in the **medulla oblongata** (decussation of pyramids).

- o   Travels down the **spinal cord to synapse on motor neurons** in the **ventral horn**.

2. Extrapyramidal Tracts

- **Function:** Controls **involuntary muscle movements, posture, and coordination**.
- Includes:
  - o   **Reticulospinal tract** (posture, walking).
  - o   **Vestibulospinal tract** (balance, head movement).
  - o   **Tectospinal tract** (head-eye coordination).

Reflex Arcs and Their Role in Involuntary Movements

A **reflex arc** is a **fast, automatic response** to a stimulus that **does not require conscious brain involvement**. Instead, it is processed **entirely in the spinal cord**.

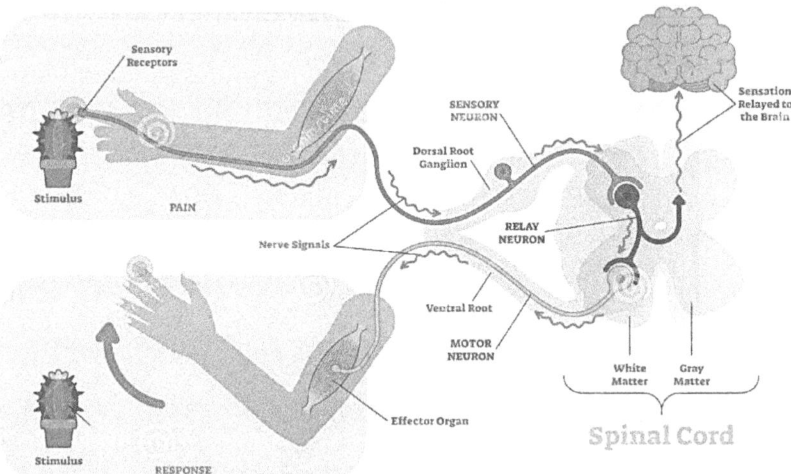

Figure 11 Reflex Arc

3.1 Components of a Reflex Arc

1. **Receptor** – Detects the stimulus (e.g., pain receptors in the skin).
2. **Sensory neuron** – Sends the signal to the spinal cord.
3. **Interneuron** – Processes the signal (may or may not be present).
4. **Motor neuron** – Sends the command to muscles.
5. **Effector (Muscle/Gland)** – Responds (e.g., pulling your hand away from a hot surface).

<ins>**3.2 Types of Reflexes**</ins>

- **Monosynaptic Reflex (e.g., Knee-Jerk Reflex)** – Involves only **one synapse** between a sensory and a motor neuron.

- **Polysynaptic Reflex (e.g., Withdrawal Reflex)** – Involves **multiple synapses** and interneurons for more complex responses.

4. Spinal Cord Injuries (SCI) and Their Effects

Spinal cord injuries can cause **partial or complete loss of sensory and motor function** below the injury level. The severity depends on the **location and extent of damage**.

4.1 Types of Spinal Cord Injuries

- **Complete SCI:** Total loss of sensation and movement below the injury.

- **Incomplete SCI:** Some function remains due to partial damage.

Injury Level	Effect
Cervical (Neck)	Quadriplegia (paralysis of arms & legs), breathing issues.
Thoracic (Upper Back)	Paraplegia (paralysis of legs), loss of bladder/bowel control.
Lumbar (Lower Back)	Weakness in legs, loss of sexual function, impaired walking.
Sacral (Pelvic Region)	Bowel, bladder, and sexual dysfunction.

4.3 Secondary Effects of SCI

- Loss of **muscle tone** (atrophy).

- **Chronic pain and spasms**.

- **Autonomic Dysreflexia** – A dangerous spike in blood pressure due to nerve dysfunction.

Peripheral Nervous System (PNS)

The **Peripheral Nervous System (PNS)** is everything **outside the brain and spinal cord**. Its main function is to **connect the central nervous system (CNS)** — the brain and spinal cord — **to the limbs and organs**.

 PNS acts like a **communication relay**, transmitting information **to and from the CNS**, allowing the body to react to external stimuli and regulate internal processes.

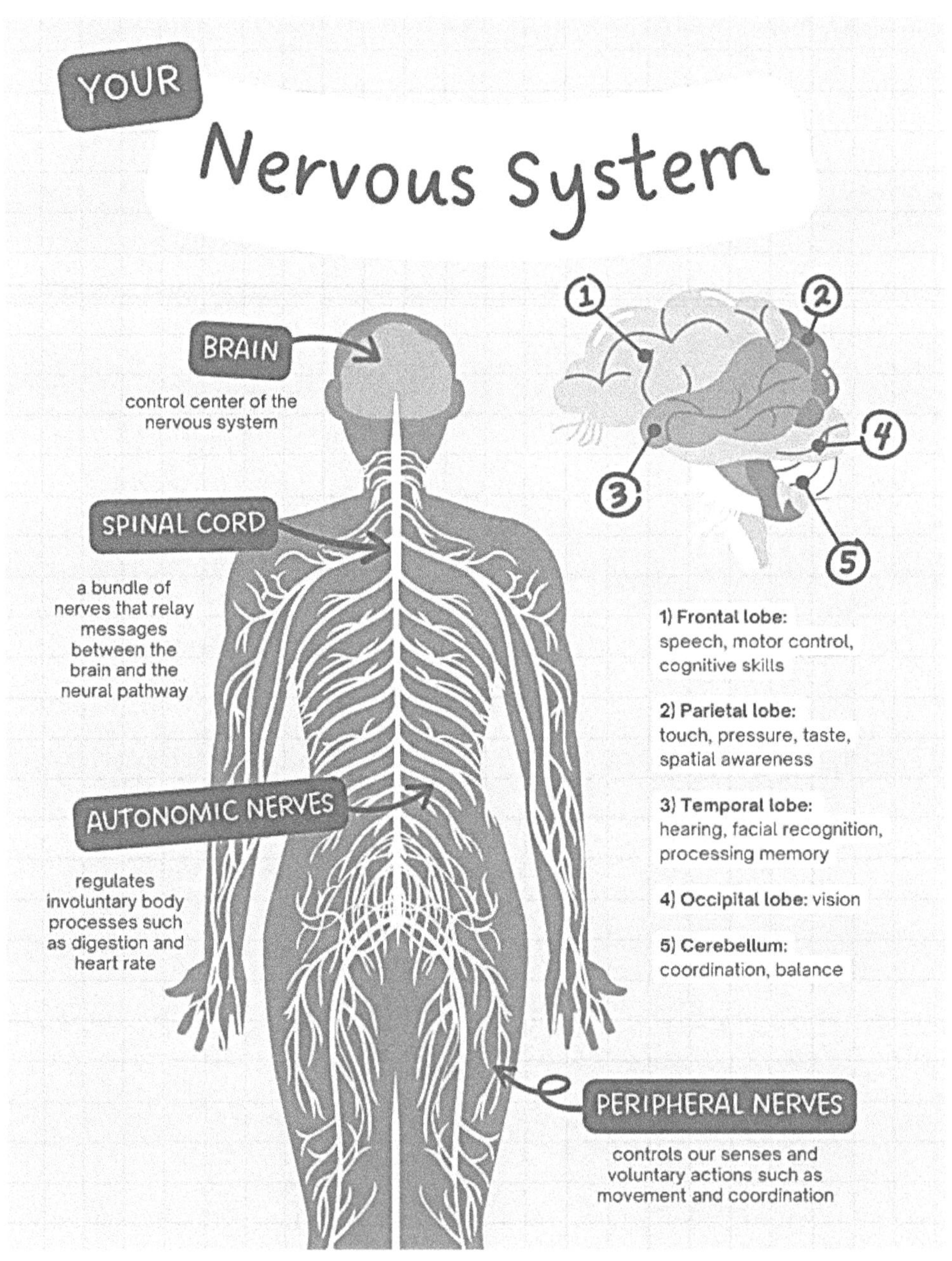

1 Somatic Nervous System (SNS)

The **Somatic Nervous System** is the **voluntary** branch of the PNS. It handles conscious movements and sensory information.

Function:

- **Voluntary control** of **skeletal muscles**.

- Receives **sensory input** from receptors in the skin, joints, and muscles.

- Sends **motor commands** from the CNS to skeletal muscles.

Includes Two Main Types of Nerves:

a) Afferent (Sensory) Nerves

- Carry **sensory information from the body to the CNS**.

- For example: pain, temperature, touch, proprioception (body position).

- Receptors in the skin/muscles detect stimuli → afferent nerves transmit to spinal cord → brain processes it.

b) Efferent (Motor) Nerves

- Carry **motor commands from CNS to the muscles**.

- E.g., deciding to move your arm → motor cortex sends signal via spinal cord → efferent nerves activate arm muscles.

Example:

When you decide to pick up a cup, the **motor cortex** sends a signal down the spinal cord, through **efferent fibers** of the SNS, activating your arm muscles. If the cup is hot, **afferent fibers** from your hand will quickly signal the brain to drop it — a reflexive and protective action.

Autonomic Nervous System (ANS)

The ANS operates automatically, outside of conscious control, and is vital for regulating the internal environment to maintain homeostasis.

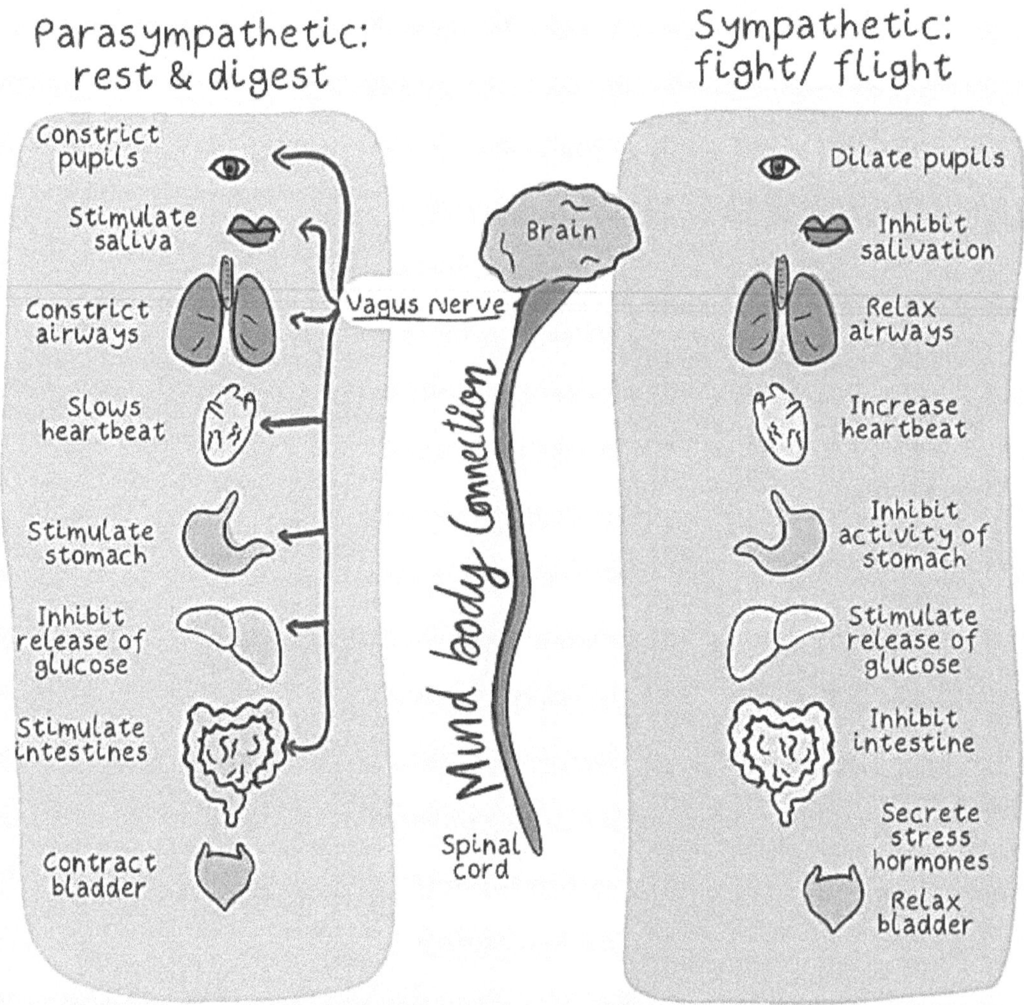

Reminder: Dorsal Vagal is an aspect of the parasympethic nervous system but a survival response

The ANS is divided into two complementary systems:

1.   **Sympathetic Nervous System – energizes the body, mobilizes for action (fight, flight, freeze)**

2.   **Parasympathetic Nervous System – conserves energy, maintains long-term health and restorative functions**

1. Sympathetic Nervous System (SNS)

The SNS prepares the body to respond to threat or challenge, increasing alertness, strength, and readiness for action. This system is thoracolumbar in origin and uses norepinephrine as its key neurotransmitter at target organs.

Major Functions of the Sympathetic System:

Function	Sympathetic Action
Heart	Increases heart rate and cardiac output
Lungs	Dilates bronchi, allows more oxygen in
Eyes	Dilates pupils (mydriasis) to improve vision
Digestive system	Inhibits digestion, reduces salivation and enzymes
Liver	Stimulates glucose release (energy boost)
Adrenal glands	Triggers secretion of epinephrine/norepinephrine
Sweat glands	Activates sweating for cooling down
Urinary bladder	Relaxes bladder, inhibits urination
Blood vessels	Constricts skin vessels, redirects blood to muscles
Muscles	Increases tension and blood supply
Reproductive system	Inhibits sexual arousal

These responses prime the body for rapid response, often at the cost of long-term health or energy conservation.

2. Parasympathetic Nervous System (PNS)

The parasympathetic system is craniosacral in origin. It promotes maintenance and recovery, slowing the body down after a stressor and supporting energy storage, digestion, and healing. Its primary neurotransmitter is acetylcholine (ACh).

Major Functions of the Parasympathetic System:

Function	Parasympathetic Action
Heart	Slows heart rate, reduces blood pressure
Lungs	Constricts bronchi, restores normal breathing
Eyes	Constricts pupils (miosis) for normal vision
Digestive system	Stimulates saliva, enzyme release, and peristalsis
Liver	Promotes glycogen storage (glucose conservation)
Bladder	Contracts bladder, enables urination
Reproductive system	Stimulates sexual arousal, erection, lubrication
Immune system	Supports immune function and repair mechanisms
Gastrointestinal tract	Enhances secretion, motility, and absorption

This system promotes deep rest, digestion, reproductive readiness, and recovery — it's vital for long-term survival.

Dual Innervation & Balance

Most organs are innervated by both sympathetic and parasympathetic branches. "dual innervation", which allows fine-tuned control depending on the situation.

Example: Heart Rate

- Sympathetic: increases HR during stress.

- Parasympathetic: slows HR when relaxed.

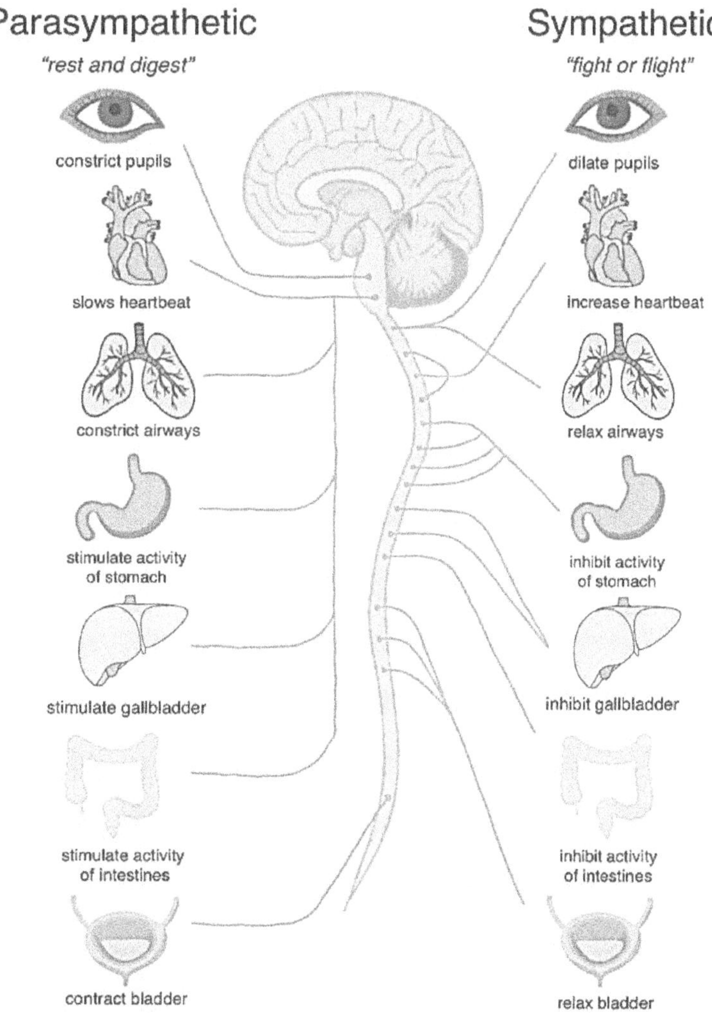

This antagonistic control allows the body to adapt dynamically to internal and external demands.

🕸 Clinical and Psychological Relevance

Situation	Dominant System	Consequences
Acute stress/anxiety	Sympathetic	Rapid HR, shallow breathing, panic
Meditation, yoga, deep breathing	Parasympathetic	Calm, improved digestion, lower HR
Chronic stress	Prolonged sympathetic	Fatigue, digestion issues, inflammation
Restorative sleep or therapy	Parasympathetic	Recovery, growth, emotional stability

Clinical Relevance

In psychological stress, the **sympathetic system is often overactive**, which can lead to:

- Anxiety

- Hypertension

- Chronic fatigue

- Insomnia

Therapies like **biofeedback, mindfulness**, and **relaxation training** aim to **enhance parasympathetic activation**, promoting calmness and recovery.

Autonomic Nervous System

/ \

Sympathetic   Parasympathetic

(Fight/Flight/Freeze)   (Rest/Digest/Repair)

Neural Transmission in the P NS

A. Action Potentials in Peripheral Nerves

An **action potential** is a rapid, temporary electrical signal that travels along the axon of a neuron. It is the primary way **neurons communicate**, allowing for transmission of sensory input and motor commands.

Steps of Action Potential Transmission:

1. **Resting Potential**:

   - Neuron is polarized (~ -70 mV).

   - More Na^+ outside, more K^+ inside the cell.

2. **Threshold Reached**:

- o   A stimulus causes depolarization.

- o   If threshold ($\sim$ -55 mV) is met, action potential fires.

3. **Depolarization**:

- o Na^+ channels open $\rightarrow$ Na^+ rushes in $\rightarrow$ inside becomes +ve.

4. **Repolarization**:

- o Na^+ channels close, K^+ channels open $\rightarrow$ K^+ exits cell.

5. **Hyperpolarization & Refractory Period**:

- o   Brief overshoot before returning to resting state.

- o   Prevents backward conduction.

6. **Propagation**:

- o   Action potential moves down the axon in an **"all-or-none"** fashion.

In **peripheral nerves**, this process allows **sensory neurons** to send information from skin/organs to the CNS and **motor neurons** to send commands from the CNS to muscles.

B. Myelination by Schwann Cells vs. Oligodendrocytes

Myelin is a **fatty insulating sheath** that speeds up action potential conduction.

- ◇ **In the PNS:**

  - • **Myelination is done by Schwann Cells**.

  - • Each Schwann cell wraps around one axon segment.

  - • Gaps between segments are called **Nodes of Ranvier**.

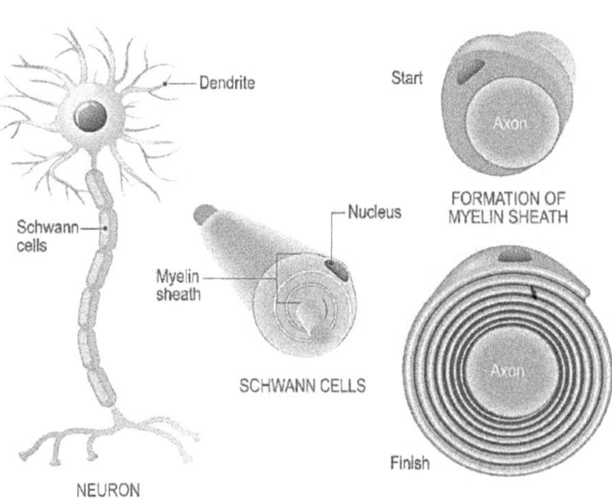

- Enables **saltatory conduction** – the action potential "jumps" from node to node → **faster** transmission.

◇ **In the CNS:**

- **Myelination is done by Oligodendrocytes**.

- Each oligodendrocyte can myelinate **multiple axons**.

- Still involves saltatory conduction, but damage (e.g., in MS) can cause severe disruption.

Saltatory Conduction:

- More efficient than continuous conduction.

- Conserves energy (less ion pumping needed).

- Especially critical for long peripheral nerves (e.g., those reaching limbs).

C. Role of Neurotransmitters in the PNS

Once the action potential reaches the **axon terminal**, communication continues via **neurotransmitters** released into the synapse.

Key Neurotransmitter: Acetylcholine (ACh)

- Most prominent neurotransmitter in the **somatic (voluntary) PNS**.

- Crucial at the **neuromuscular junction (NMJ)**:

  ○ Junction between a **motor neuron and a skeletal muscle fiber**.

Neuromuscular Transmission Process:

1. **Action potential reaches terminal of motor neuron.**

2. **Voltage-gated Ca^{2+} channels open**, Ca^{2+} enters.

3. Vesicles release **acetylcholine (ACh)** into synaptic cleft.

4. ACh binds to **nicotinic receptors** on muscle fiber membrane.

5. Causes **depolarization** of muscle cell → **muscle contraction**.

6. ACh is rapidly broken down by **acetylcholinesterase (AChE)**.

Autonomic PNS Neurotransmitters:

Autonomic Division	Preganglionic NT	Postganglionic NT	Target Effects
Sympathetic	ACh	Norepinephrine	Fight-or-flight
Parasympathetic	ACh	ACh	Rest-and-digest

- **Sympathetic**: Mobilizes energy, increases HR, dilates pupils.

- **Parasympathetic**: Conserves energy, slows HR, promotes digestion.

Clinical Insights:

- **Demyelinating disorders** (like **Guillain-Barré Syndrome** in the PNS or **Multiple Sclerosis** in the CNS) damage insulation, slowing or blocking conduction.

- **Botox** blocks ACh release → prevents muscle contraction.

- **Myasthenia Gravis**: Autoimmune attack on ACh receptors at the NMJ → muscle weakness.

Neuroanatomy and Functional Mapping

A. Nerve Pathways and Their Functional Maps

The **PNS** consists of cranial and spinal nerves, which form **sensory (afferent)** and **motor (efferent)** pathways connecting the body to the CNS. Understanding these nerve pathways helps map how **specific sensations or motor commands** travel.

◇ **Sensory Pathways (Afferent):**

- Information flows **from receptors (skin, muscles, organs)** to the CNS.

- Signals travel via **dorsal roots of spinal nerves** or **cranial nerves**.

- Example: Touch receptors in the skin send signals through the **spinothalamic tract** to the brain.

◇ **Motor Pathways (Efferent):**

- Instructions flow **from the brain to effectors (muscles or glands)**.

- Travel via **ventral roots** of spinal nerves or motor cranial nerves.

- Example: The **corticospinal tract** carries voluntary motor commands from the motor cortex to limbs.

These pathways are mapped **somatotopically**, meaning different body parts correspond to specific brain regions (like in the motor/sensory homunculus).

B. Reflex Arcs: Integration of CNS and PNS

A **reflex arc** is a fast, automatic, involuntary response to a stimulus, often occurring **without conscious brain involvement**.

Basic Components of a Reflex Arc:

1. **Sensory Receptor** – Detects stimulus (e.g., pain, stretch).

2. **Afferent Neuron** – Carries signal to spinal cord.

3. **Interneuron** (in spinal cord) – Integrates information (CNS component).

4. **Efferent Neuron** – Sends command to effector.

5. **Effector** – Muscle or gland responds (e.g., contracts or secretes).

Example:

Knee-jerk reflex (patellar reflex):

- Tap on patellar tendon stretches muscle.

- Sensory input travels to spinal cord.

- Motor output immediately contracts the muscle → leg kicks.

Note: Reflexes ensure survival and postural control and are critical for neurologic testing (used clinically to assess spinal integrity).

C. PNS Damage and Regeneration

Damage to PNS:

- Often results from trauma, compression, diabetes (neuropathy), infections, or autoimmune attacks.

- Can lead to:

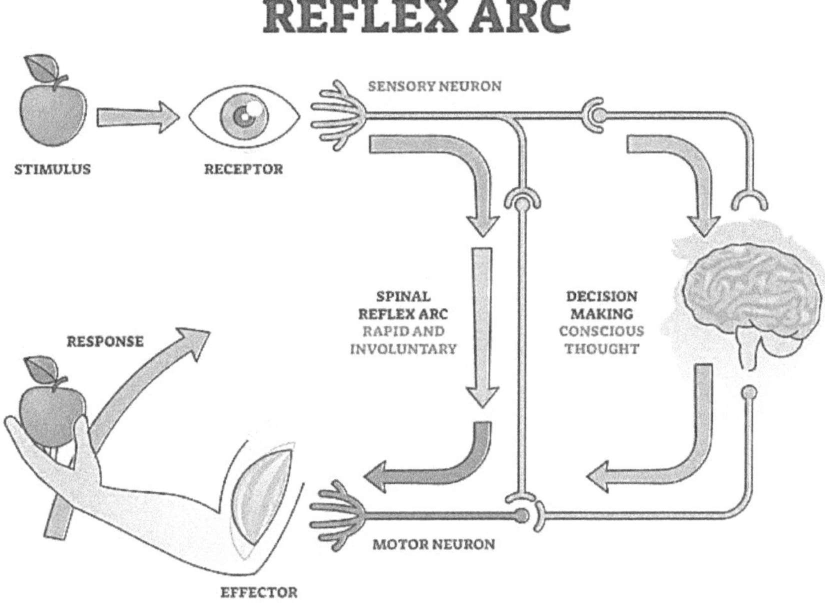

- Sensory loss (numbness, tingling).

- Motor dysfunction (paralysis or weakness).

- Autonomic disruption (heart rate, digestion issues).

Regeneration Potential in PNS:

- **PNS neurons can regenerate**, unlike CNS neurons.

- **Schwann cells** play a vital role:

- Guide axon regrowth by forming **regeneration tubes**.

- Secrete growth factors.

- **Axons can regrow** at ~1-3 mm/day if the neuron cell body is intact.

In contrast, CNS damage (due to oligodendrocyte inhibition, lack of growth cues, glial scarring) rarely heals naturally.

D. Clinical Insights: Role of PNS in Disorders

1. Peripheral Neuropathy:

- Common in diabetes, alcohol abuse, infections (e.g., shingles), or toxins.

- Symptoms: Pain, burning, loss of sensation or coordination.

2. Autonomic Dysfunction:

- Seen in Parkinson's disease, diabetes, or spinal cord injuries.

- Disrupts regulation of HR, BP, digestion, or temperature.

- May cause **orthostatic hypotension**, **gastroparesis**, etc.

3. Spinal Cord Injury:

- Often damages **both CNS and PNS pathways**.

- Sensory and motor loss depends on injury level:

  - Cervical = tetraplegia

  - Thoracic/Lumbar = paraplegia

- Reflex arcs may remain intact below lesion level (e.g., spasticity due to loss of descending inhibition).

Summary Table:

Aspect	Explanation
Sensory (Afferent) Pathway	Body → CNS via dorsal root
Motor (Efferent) Pathway	CNS → Body via ventral root

Reflex Arc	Involves receptor → sensory → spinal integration → motor → effector
Regeneration in PNS	Schwann cells guide axon regrowth
Clinical Examples	Peripheral neuropathy, autonomic failure, spinal injuries

ENDOCRINE SYSTEM

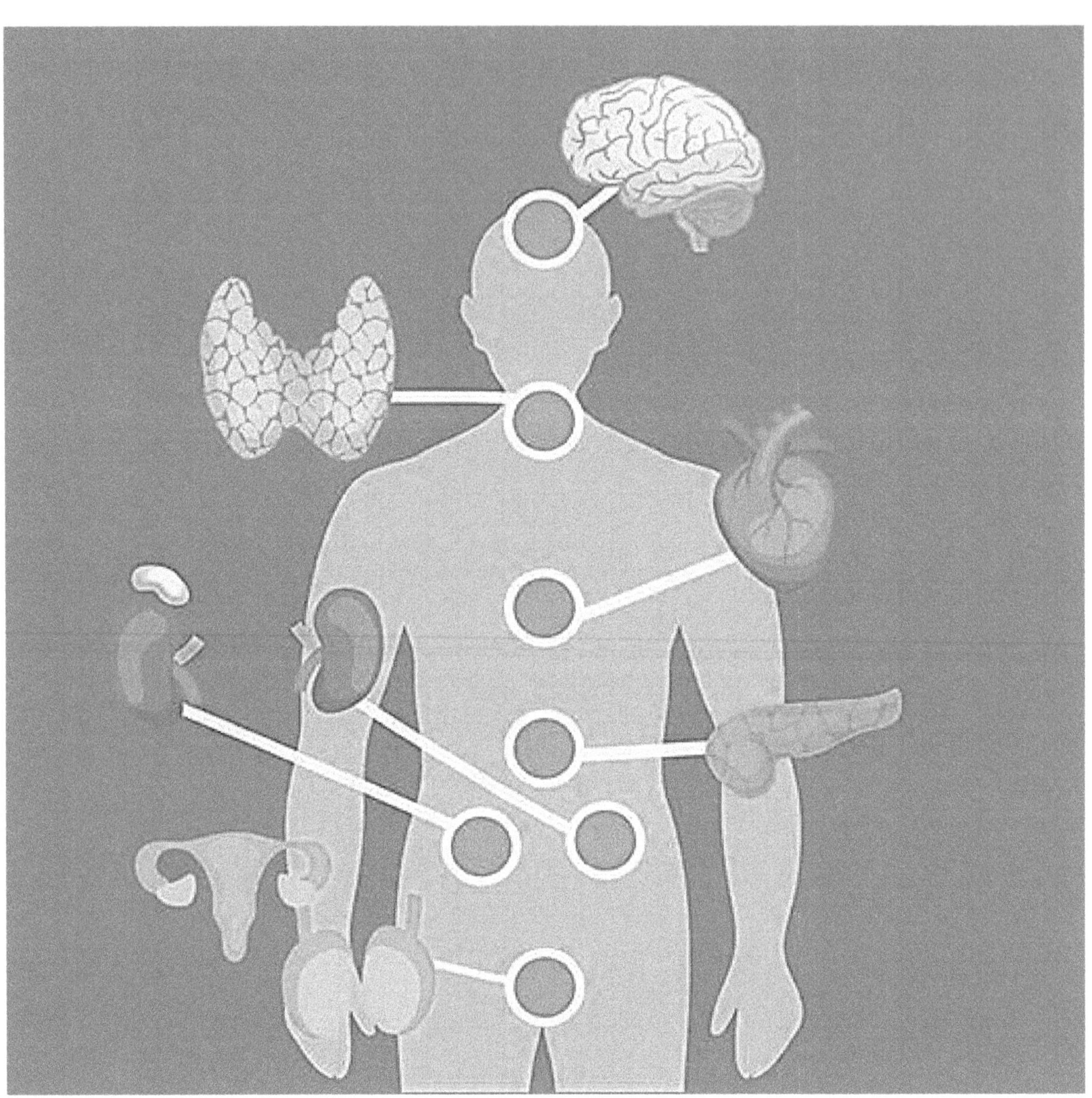

Endocrine Glands

The endocrine glands are a vital part of the human body's **endocrine system**, which is responsible for regulating various physiological functions through the secretion of **hormones**. Unlike exocrine glands, which release their secretions through ducts, endocrine glands are **ductless** and release hormones directly into the **bloodstream**. These hormones help control growth, metabolism, reproduction, and homeostasis.

The major endocrine glands include:

- **Pituitary gland** – The "master gland" that regulates other glands.

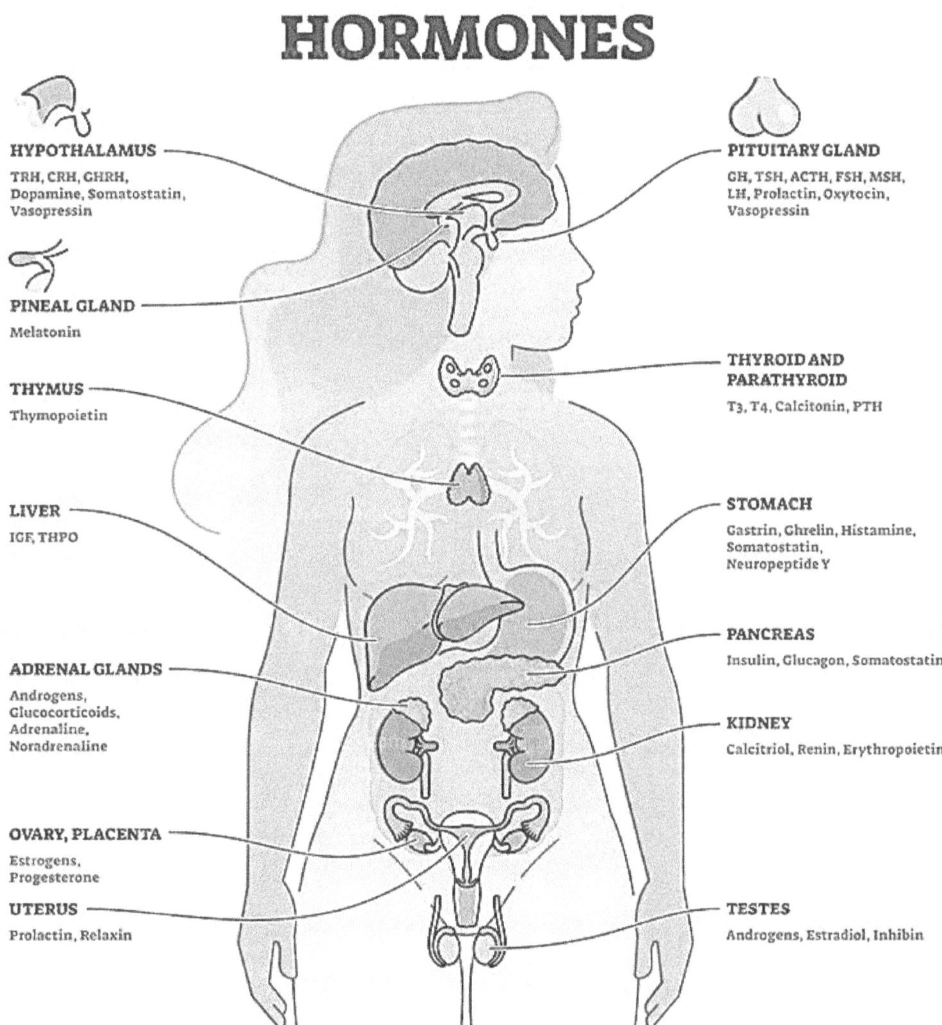

- **Thyroid gland** – Controls metabolism and energy production.

- **Parathyroid glands** – Regulate calcium levels in the body.

- **Adrenal glands** – Produce stress hormones like cortisol and adrenaline.

- **Pancreas** – Regulates blood sugar levels through insulin and glucagon.

- **Pineal gland** – Influences sleep-wake cycles through melatonin.

- **Gonads (Ovaries & Testes)** – Regulate reproductive functions and secondary sexual characteristics.

The endocrine system works in coordination with the **nervous system** to ensure proper body functioning. Any imbalance in hormone production can lead to disorders such as diabetes, thyroid dysfunction, or hormonal imbalances, affecting overall health.

The Pituitary Gland: The Master Regulator

The **pituitary gland** is often referred to as the **"master gland"** because of its central role in regulating various physiological functions by controlling other endocrine glands. It is a **pea-sized structure** located at the base of the brain, just below the hypothalamus, to which it is connected via the **infundibulum (pituitary stalk)**. This connection allows the hypothalamus to regulate pituitary activity, making it a key player in the **neuroendocrine system**.

Pituitary gland

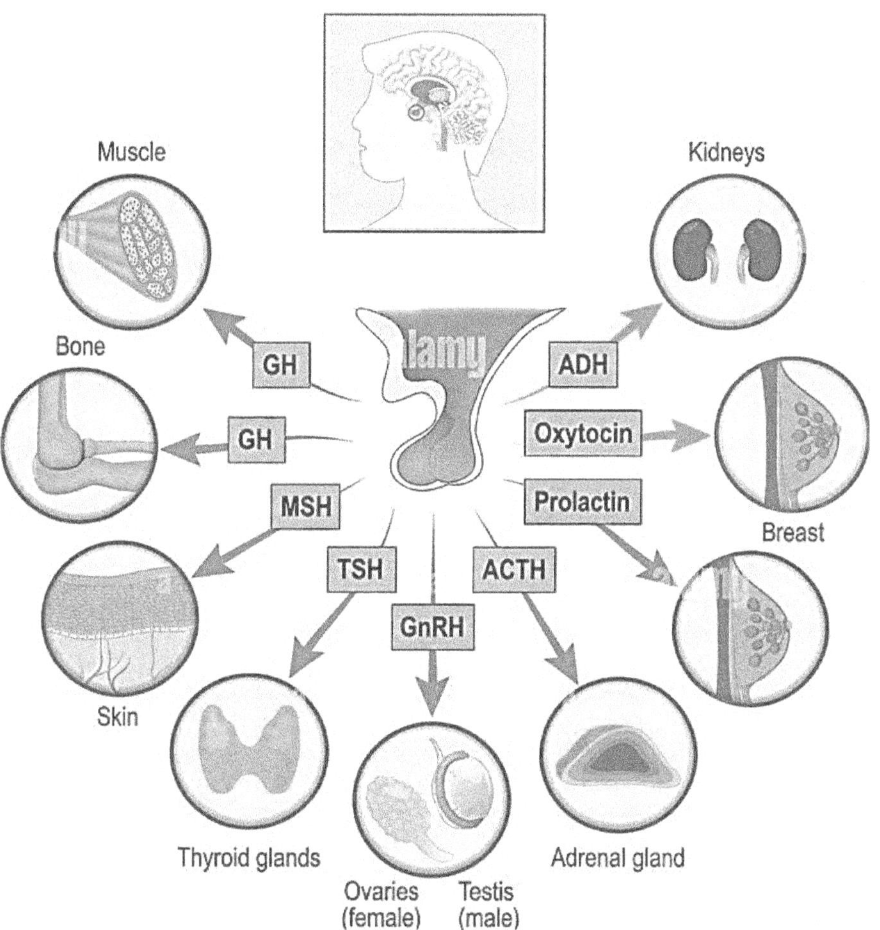

Structure and Divisions of the Pituitary Gland

The pituitary gland consists of two distinct lobes that function differently:

1. **Anterior Pituitary (Adenohypophysis)** – Produces and secretes hormones that regulate growth, metabolism, reproduction, and stress responses. It functions under the control of the hypothalamus, which releases **releasing and inhibiting hormones** through the **hypophyseal portal system**.

2. **Posterior Pituitary (Neurohypophysis)** – Stores and releases hormones produced by the hypothalamus, particularly **oxytocin** and **vasopressin (antidiuretic hormone, ADH)**. Unlike the anterior pituitary, it does not synthesize its own hormones.

Hormones Secreted by the Pituitary Gland

Anterior Pituitary Hormones **(Controlled by Hypothalamus):**

- **Growth Hormone (GH)** – Regulates growth, cell regeneration, and metabolism. Deficiency can cause **dwarfism**, while excess can lead to **gigantism** or **acromegaly**.

- **Adrenocorticotropic Hormone (ACTH)** – Stimulates the adrenal cortex to release cortisol, crucial for stress response.

- **Thyroid-Stimulating Hormone (TSH)** – Controls thyroid gland activity, regulating metabolism and energy balance.

- **Luteinizing Hormone (LH) & Follicle-Stimulating Hormone (FSH)** – Key in reproductive function, stimulating ovaries and testes to produce sex hormones.

- **Prolactin (PRL)** – Regulates milk production in females postpartum.

Posterior Pituitary Hormones **(Stored & Released, Not Produced Here):**

- **Oxytocin** – Facilitates uterine contractions during childbirth and bonding behaviours.

- **Vasopressin (Antidiuretic Hormone, ADH)** – Helps regulate water balance in the body by controlling kidney function.

2. Functional Divisions of the Pituitary Gland

A. Anterior Pituitary (Adenohypophysis)

The **anterior pituitary** is the larger portion and is responsible for producing and releasing hormones. Its function is **regulated by the hypothalamus** through the **hypophyseal portal system**, a network of blood vessels that transports **releasing and inhibiting hormones** from the hypothalamus to the pituitary.

Hormones Secreted by the Anterior Pituitary:

1. **Growth Hormone (GH) / Somatotropin**

   - Stimulates body growth by promoting **cell division, protein synthesis, and bone elongation**.

- o Regulated by **Growth Hormone-Releasing Hormone (GHRH)** and **Somatostatin (GH-inhibiting hormone, GHIH)** from the hypothalamus.

- o Excess GH causes **gigantism** (before puberty) or **acromegaly** (after puberty), while a deficiency causes **dwarfism**.

2. **Thyroid-Stimulating Hormone (TSH) / Thyrotropin**

- o Stimulates the thyroid gland to produce **thyroxine (T4) and triiodothyronine (T3)**, which regulate metabolism.

- o Controlled by **Thyrotropin-Releasing Hormone (TRH)** from the hypothalamus.

- o TSH deficiency leads to **hypothyroidism**, while excess causes **hyperthyroidism**.

3. **Adrenocorticotropic Hormone (ACTH) / Corticotropin**

- o Stimulates the **adrenal cortex** to secrete **glucocorticoids (e.g., cortisol)**, which help manage stress and metabolism.

- o Controlled by **Corticotropin-Releasing Hormone (CRH)** from the hypothalamus.

- o Excess ACTH leads to **Cushing's disease**, while deficiency results in **adrenal insufficiency**.

4. **Luteinizing Hormone (LH) and Follicle-Stimulating Hormone (FSH)** (Gonadotropins)

- o **LH**: Triggers ovulation in females and stimulates testosterone production in males.

- o **FSH**: Promotes follicle development in ovaries and spermatogenesis in testes.

- o Both are regulated by **Gonadotropin-Releasing Hormone (GnRH)**.

- o Deficiencies result in **infertility or delayed puberty**.

5. **Prolactin (PRL)**

- o Stimulates **milk production (lactation)** in females after childbirth.

- o Suppressed by **dopamine (Prolactin Inhibitory Hormone, PIH)** from the hypothalamus.

- o Hyperprolactinemia (excess PRL) can cause **infertility, irregular menstruation, and decreased libido**.

B. Posterior Pituitary (Neurohypophysis)

The **posterior pituitary** does not produce its own hormones but stores and releases two **neurohormones** produced by the hypothalamus:

1. **Oxytocin**

   - Induces **uterine contractions** during labor and stimulates **milk ejection** during breastfeeding.

   - Plays a role in **bonding, trust, and emotional attachment**.

   - Administered medically to **induce labor**.

2. **Vasopressin (Antidiuretic Hormone, ADH)**

   - Regulates **water balance** by acting on the kidneys to **reduce urine output** and prevent dehydration.

   - Deficiency leads to **Diabetes Insipidus**, characterized by excessive thirst and urination.

3. Regulation of the Pituitary Gland

The **hypothalamic-pituitary axis** (HPA) regulates the pituitary gland through a **negative feedback mechanism**, ensuring hormonal balance.

- For example, when **cortisol levels** rise, the **hypothalamus reduces CRH production**, leading to **lower ACTH release** from the pituitary. This **inhibits excess cortisol production** from the adrenal glands.

- Similar feedback loops exist for **thyroid hormones (T3/T4)** and **sex hormones (estrogen/testosterone)**.

4. Clinical Disorders of the Pituitary Gland

Pituitary dysfunction can have **widespread effects** due to its regulatory role.

1. **Hypopituitarism** (Low hormone production)

   - Causes: Tumors, head injury, infections, or genetic mutations.

- o Symptoms: Fatigue, weight gain, reproductive issues, and growth impairment.

2. **Hyperpituitarism** (Excess hormone production)

- o **Cushing's Disease**: Excess ACTH → **High cortisol**, leading to weight gain, high BP, and diabetes.

- o **Acromegaly/Gigantism**: Excess GH → **Exaggerated growth** of bones and tissues.

- o **Hyperprolactinemia**: Excess PRL → **Irregular menstruation, infertility, and lactation in non-pregnant individuals**.

3. **Diabetes Insipidus** (Low ADH production)

- o Symptoms: Excessive thirst and urination.

- o Causes: Damage to the hypothalamus/posterior pituitary.

5. Importance of the Pituitary Gland in Psychology

The **pituitary gland is essential for psychological well-being** because:

- It regulates **stress hormones (cortisol)**, which influence **anxiety, depression, and cognitive function**.

- Oxytocin plays a role in **bonding, love, and social interactions**.

PINEAL GLAND

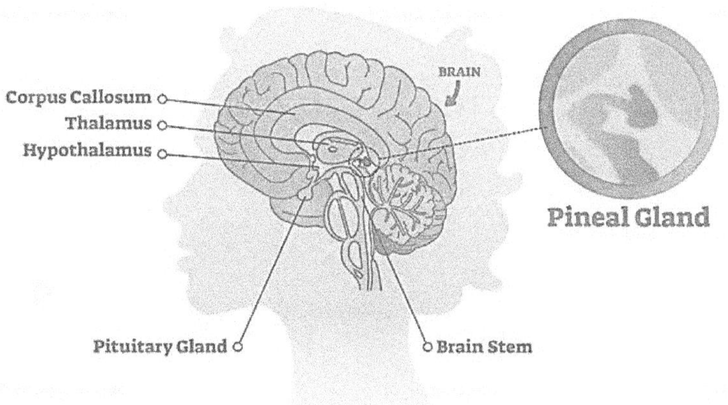

- GH and thyroid hormones impact **mood, energy levels, and mental clarity**.

Psychologists and neuroscientists study the **pituitary's role in mental health disorders** like depression, anxiety, and PTSD, where **hormonal imbalances** may contribute to symptoms.

The **pituitary gland** is a **central regulator** of the endocrine system, influencing growth, metabolism, reproduction, and stress response. It functions in close coordination with the **hypothalamus** and other glands.

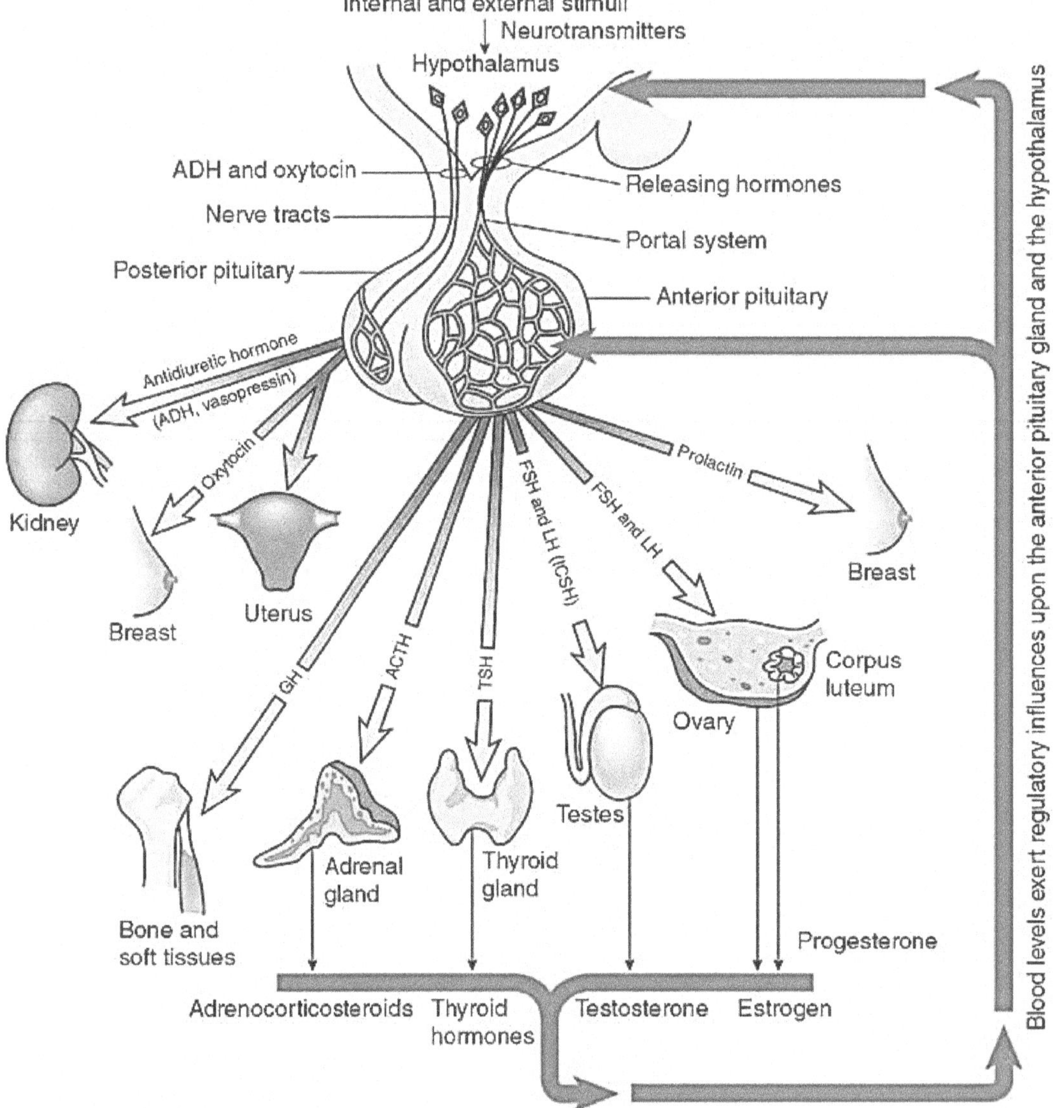

1. Hypothalamus: The Neuroendocrine Control Centre

Location: Base of the brain, above the pituitary gland.

Function: Acts as a **link between the nervous system and endocrine system**, controlling hormone release from the **pituitary gland** via releasing and inhibiting hormones.

Major Hypothalamic Hormones:

- **Corticotropin-Releasing Hormone (CRH)** → Stimulates ACTH release from pituitary (stress response).

- **Gonadotropin-Releasing Hormone (GnRH)** → Stimulates LH & FSH secretion (reproductive function).

- **Thyrotropin-Releasing Hormone (TRH)** → Stimulates TSH secretion (thyroid regulation).

- **Growth Hormone-Releasing Hormone (GHRH)** → Stimulates GH secretion (growth & metabolism).

- **Somatostatin (GHIH)** → Inhibits GH and TSH release.

- **Dopamine (Prolactin Inhibitory Hormone, PIH)** → Inhibits prolactin release.

<u>**Psychological Impact:**</u>

- **Regulates emotions, appetite, stress, and sexual behaviour** via connections to the **limbic system**.

- Dysfunction can lead to **depression, anxiety, eating disorders, and hormonal imbalances**.

2. Pineal Gland: Sleep-Wake Regulation

Location: Deep in the brain, near the thalamus.

Function: Produces **melatonin**, a hormone that regulates **circadian rhythms** (biological clock).

Hormone Secreted:

- **Melatonin** → Released in response to darkness, inducing sleep.

Psychological Impact:

- Melatonin imbalances are linked to **insomnia, depression, and seasonal affective disorder (SAD)**.

- Light exposure (especially blue light from screens) suppresses melatonin, disrupting sleep.

Thyroid and Parathyroid Glands

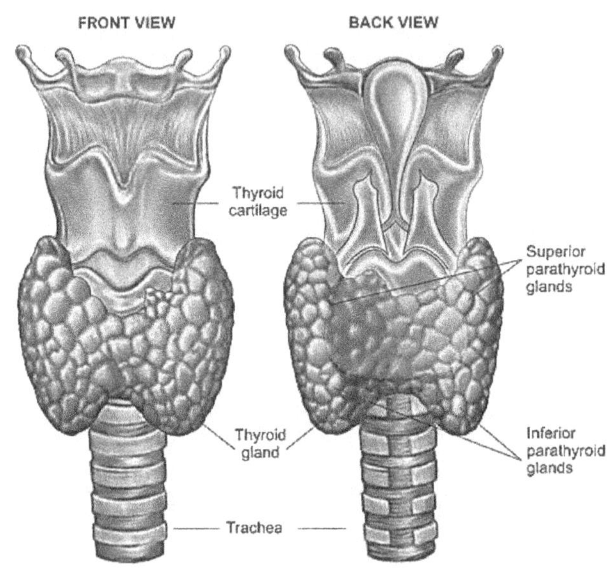

3. Thyroid Gland: Metabolic and Growth Control

Location: Neck, around the trachea.

Function: Regulates **metabolism, energy production, growth, and development**.

Hormones Secreted:

1. **Thyroxine (T4) and Triiodothyronine (T3)**

   o   Increase **metabolic rate, oxygen consumption, and heat production**.

   o   Essential for **brain development, muscle function, and heart rate regulation**.

2. **Calcitonin**

   o   Lowers blood calcium levels by inhibiting bone breakdown.

Disorders:

- **Hypothyroidism (Low T3/T4 levels):** Fatigue, weight gain, depression, slow metabolism.

- **Hyperthyroidism (High T3/T4 levels):** Weight loss, anxiety, high heart rate, excessive energy.

Psychological Impact:

- **Thyroid disorders are linked to depression, anxiety, cognitive dysfunction, and mood swings.**

4. Parathyroid Glands: Calcium Homeostasis

Location: Four small glands behind the thyroid.

Function: Regulates **calcium levels in blood** for nerve and muscle function.

Hormone Secreted:

- **Parathyroid Hormone (PTH)** → Increases blood calcium by promoting bone resorption and calcium absorption from intestines.

Disorders:

- **Hypoparathyroidism:** Muscle cramps, seizures, brittle bones.

- **Hyperparathyroidism:** Kidney stones, bone loss, muscle weakness.

Psychological Impact:

- Calcium imbalances can cause **irritability, depression, and cognitive issues**.

5. Adrenal Glands: Stress Response and Metabolism

Adrenal Medulla

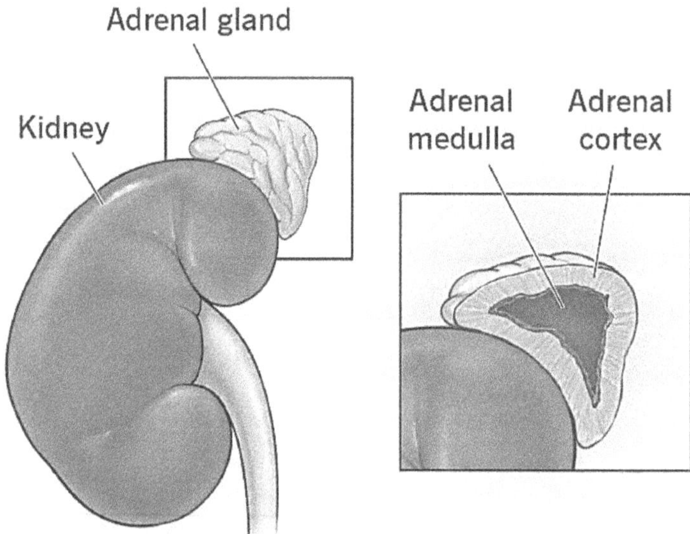

Location: On top of the kidneys.

Function: Regulates **stress response, metabolism, blood pressure, and immune function**.

Divisions of Adrenal Glands:

A. Adrenal Cortex (Outer Layer) – Steroid Hormones

- **Cortisol** (Glucocorticoid) → Regulates **stress response, metabolism, and inflammation**.

- **Aldosterone** (Mineralocorticoid) → Controls **salt & water balance, blood pressure**.

- **Androgens** (Sex hormones) → Secondary sexual characteristics.

B. Adrenal Medulla (Inner Layer) – Fight-or-Flight Hormones

- **Epinephrine (Adrenaline) & Norepinephrine** → Increase heart rate, energy, alertness during stress.

Disorders:

- **Cushing's Syndrome (Excess cortisol):** Weight gain, high BP, anxiety, insomnia.

- **Addison's Disease (Low cortisol):** Fatigue, low BP, depression.

Psychological Impact:

- Chronic stress & excess cortisol contribute to **anxiety, depression, and memory impairment**.

6. Pancreas: Blood Sugar Regulation

Location: Behind the stomach.

Function: Regulates **glucose levels** for energy balance.

Hormones Secreted from Islets of Langerhans (alpha, beta and delta):

- **Insulin** → Lowers blood sugar by promoting glucose uptake into cells.

- **Glucagon** → Raises blood sugar by breaking down glycogen.

- **Somatostatin-** controls the release of other hormones

Disorders:

- **Diabetes Mellitus (Insulin Deficiency or Resistance):** High blood sugar, fatigue, organ damage.

- **Hypoglycemia (Low Blood Sugar):** Confusion, irritability, fainting.

Psychological Impact:

- Blood sugar fluctuations can cause **mood swings, cognitive decline, and fatigue**.

7. Gonads (Testes & Ovaries): Reproductive Hormones

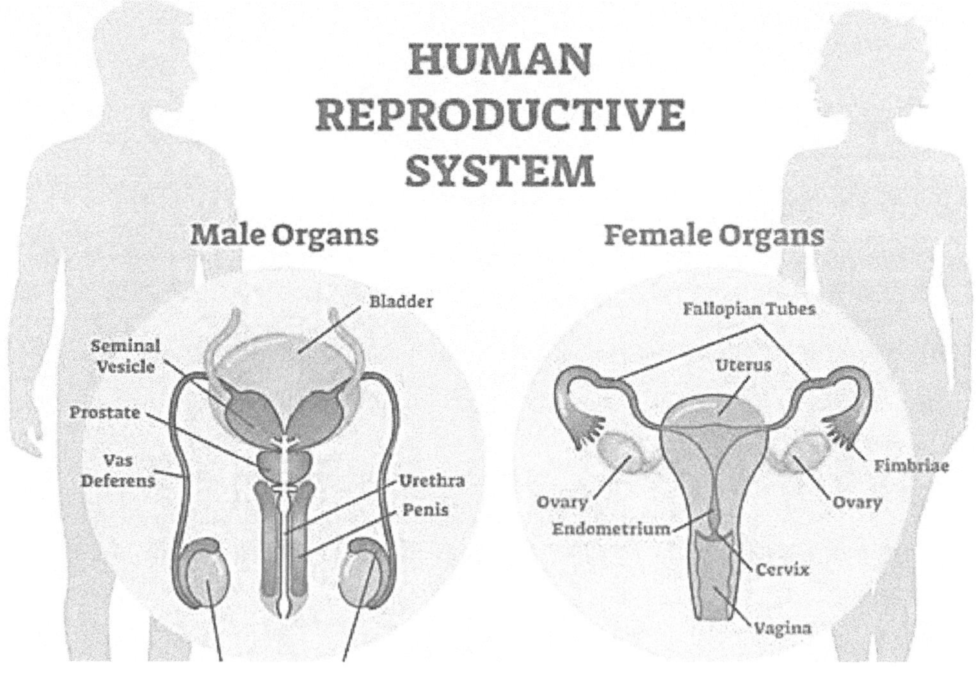

Location:

- **Testes (Males)** – In scrotum.

- **Ovaries (Females)** – Lower abdomen.

Function: Regulate **sexual development, reproduction, and secondary sexual characteristics**.

Hormones Secreted:

1. **Testosterone (Testes)** → Male puberty, muscle mass, libido.

2. **Estrogen (Ovaries)** → Female puberty, menstruation, mood regulation.

3. **Progesterone (Ovaries)** → Pregnancy support, menstrual cycle control.

Psychological Impact:

- Hormonal imbalances can lead to **mood disorders, depression, aggression, or anxiety**.

8. Thymus Gland: Immune System Development

Location: Behind the sternum (shrinks after puberty).
Function: Produces **T-cells for immune defense**.

Hormone Secreted:

- **Thymosin** → Stimulates T-cell development.

Psychological Impact:

- Weak immune function can increase **stress, fatigue, and susceptibility to illness**.

Regulation and Importance

The **pituitary gland does not function independently**. It is tightly regulated by the **hypothalamus**, which releases specific releasing and inhibiting hormones to control anterior pituitary function. For example:

- **Corticotropin-releasing hormone (CRH)** stimulates ACTH release, leading to cortisol production.

- **Thyrotropin-releasing hormone (TRH)** stimulates TSH, which activates the thyroid gland.

Thymus Gland

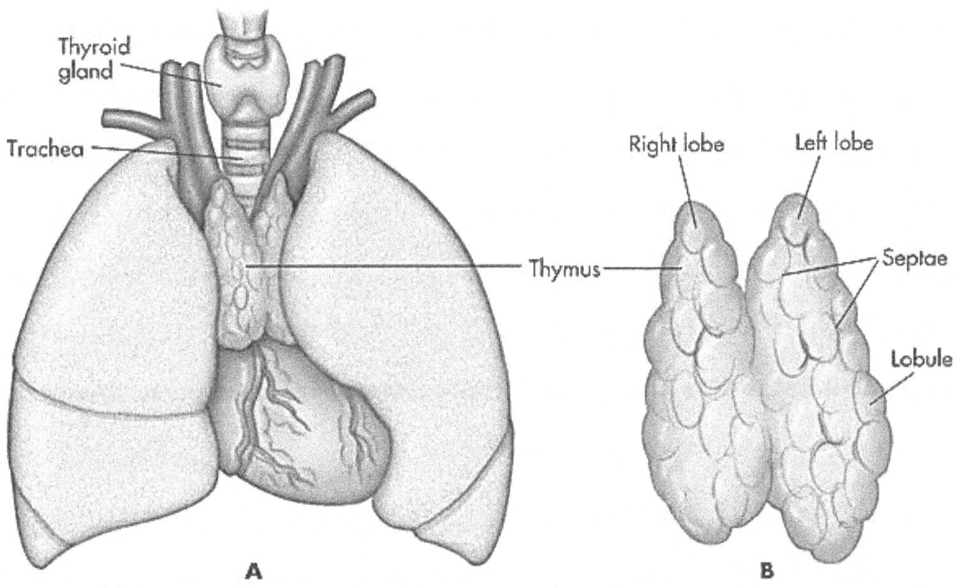

- **Gonadotropin-releasing hormone (GnRH)** controls LH and FSH secretion.

This **feedback loop system** ensures hormonal balance and prevents excessive secretion of hormones, maintaining homeostasis.

The **pituitary gland** plays a critical role in maintaining the body's **hormonal balance, stress response, metabolism, reproduction, and growth**. It is essential for overall health and is **tightly controlled by the hypothalamus through feedback mechanisms**. Any dysfunction in this gland can have widespread physiological consequences, making it a key focus in **both psychology and medical research**.

BASIC PHYSIOLOGICAL SENSES: VISUAL AND AUDITORY

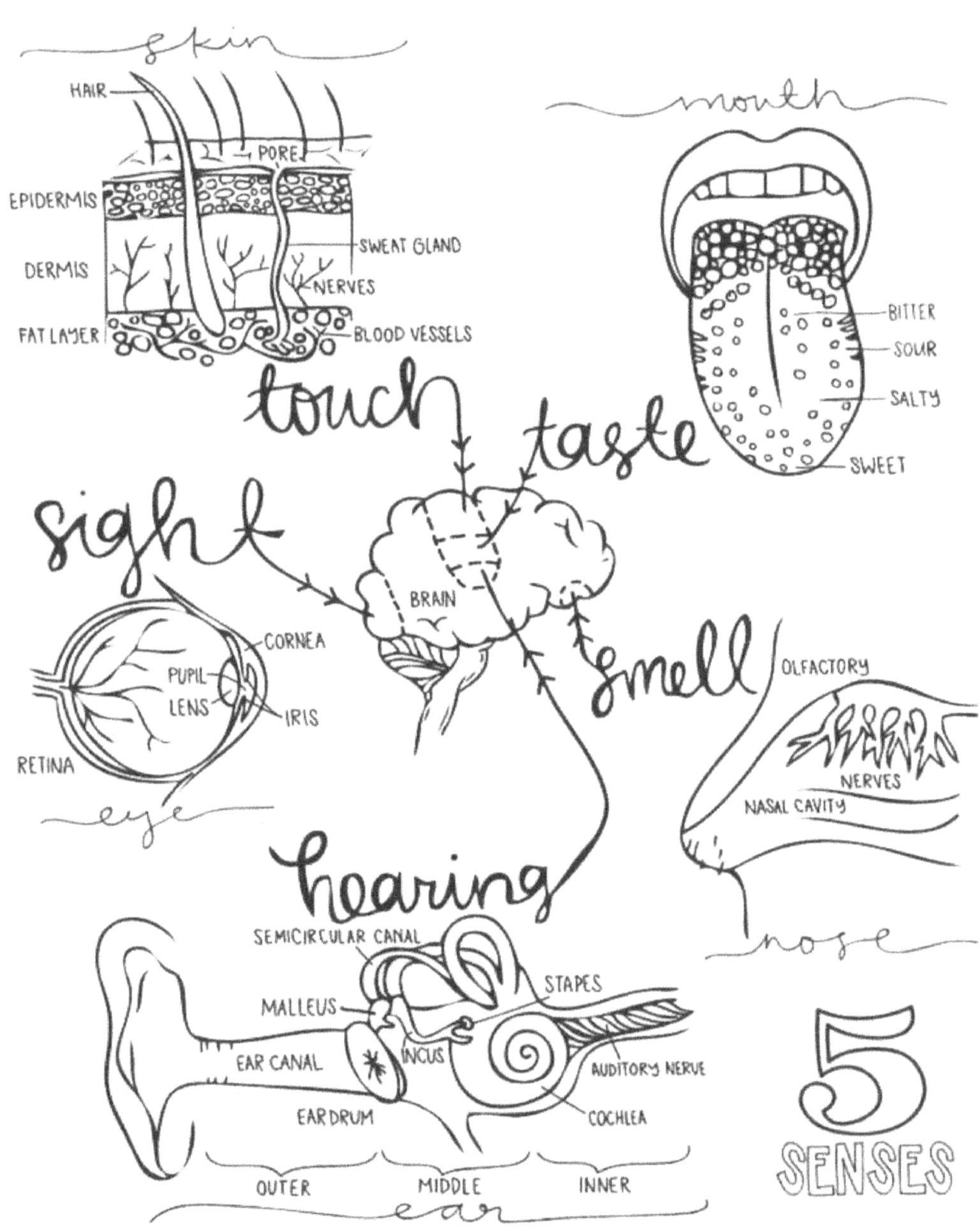

Visual Sense

Vision, or the ability to perceive and interpret the environment through light, is one of the most complex and vital sensory processes. It involves the conversion of light signals into neural impulses, which are then interpreted by the brain to create visual experiences. Vision is not only a sensory process but also plays a crucial role in behaviour, movement, and cognition.

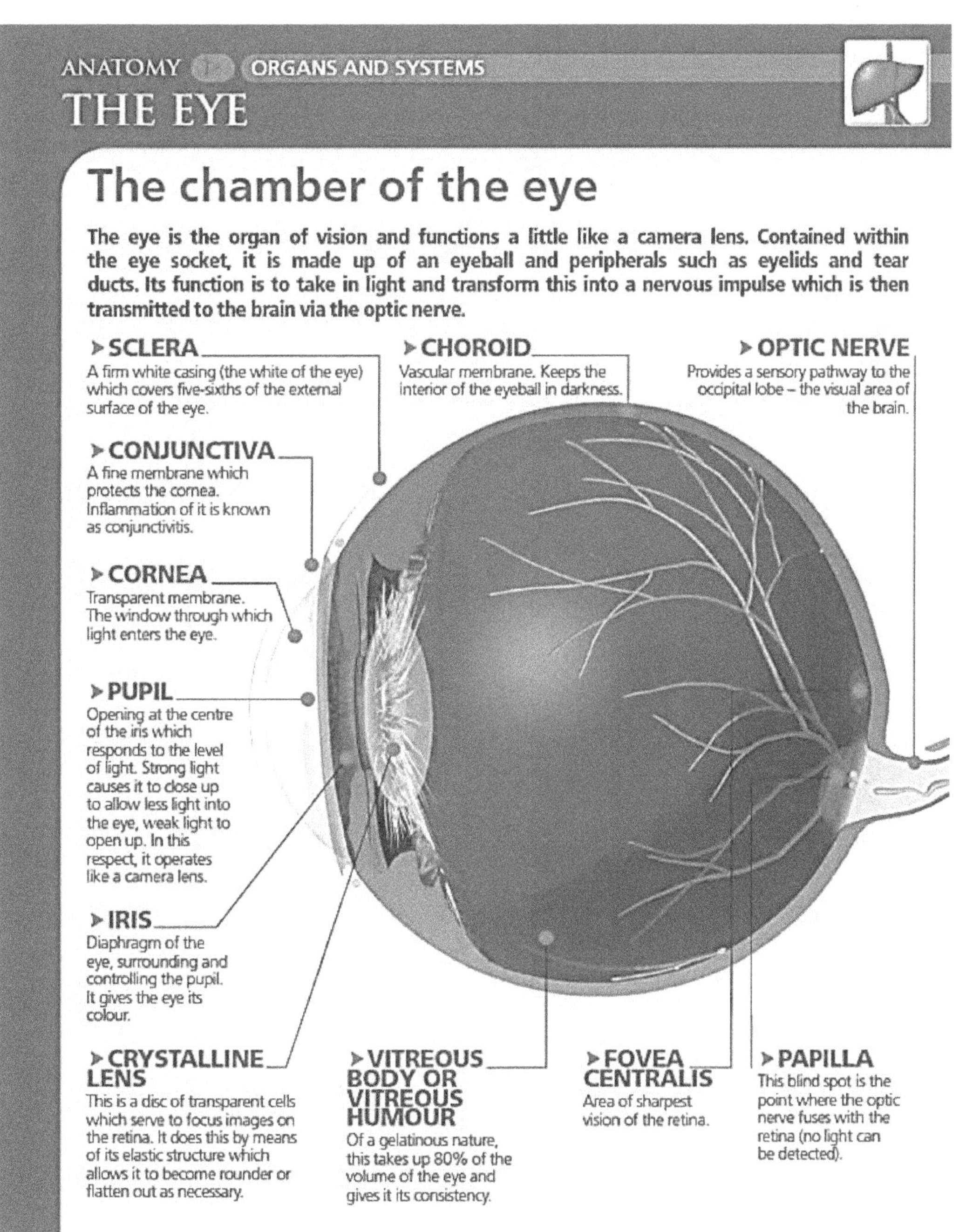

1. The Visual Pathway

The process of vision can be broken down into several stages, from the reception of light by the eyes to the processing of visual information by the brain.

- **Light Reception**: Light enters the eye, where it is refracted by the cornea and focused by the lens onto the retina.

- **Transduction**: The retina contains photoreceptor cells (rods and cones) that transduce light into electrical signals.

- **Transmission to the Brain**: The optic nerve carries the electrical signals from the retina to the brain.

- **Visual Processing**: The visual information is processed by the brain, particularly in the primary visual cortex (V1) in the occipital lobe, where different visual features (e.g., shape, color, motion) are interpreted.

2. Structures Involved in Vision

A. The Eye: Key Anatomical Structures

1. **Cornea**: The transparent, outermost layer of the eye that helps focus light entering the eye.

   - Functions as a protective barrier and refracts light.

2. **Pupil**: The black circular opening in the center of the iris.

   - Regulates the amount of light entering the eye (pupillary reflex).

3. **Iris**: The colored part of the eye, responsible for controlling the size of the pupil.

   - Adjusts the pupil size in response to light intensity (dilates in low light, constricts in bright light).

4. **Lens**: A transparent structure located behind the iris that helps focus light on the retina.

   - Changes shape (accommodation) to focus on objects at different distances.

5. **Retina**: The light-sensitive layer at the back of the eye that contains photoreceptors (rods and cones).

   o   The retina transduces light into neural signals.

6. **Fovea**: A small pit located in the center of the retina, responsible for sharp central vision.

   o   Contains a high concentration of cones and is crucial for tasks requiring fine detail, such as reading or recognizing faces.

7. **Optic Nerve**: The bundle of nerve fibers that carries visual information from the retina to the brain.

   o   Transmits electrical signals to the brain for further processing.

B. Photoreceptors: Rods and Cones

1. **Rods**:

o   Responsible for vision in low-light conditions (scotopic vision).

o   Located primarily in the periphery of the retina.

o   More sensitive to light but do not detect color (monochromatic vision).

2. **Cones**:

o   Responsible for color vision and visual acuity (photopic vision).

o   Located mainly in the fovea.

o   Three types of cones: S-cones (sensitive to short wavelengths, blue), M-cones (green), and L-cones (red).

o   Cones enable the brain to perceive a wide range of colors through color mixing and wavelength detection.

Transduction: Conversion of Light into Neural Signals

- **Phototransduction**: This is the process by which photoreceptors convert light into electrical signals.

- In the Rods: When light hits the rod cells, a biochemical cascade is triggered that leads to the closure of sodium channels, hyperpolarizing the cell and decreasing neurotransmitter release. This leads to the generation of electrical signals that are transmitted to the brain.

- In the Cones: Similar to rods, but with different visual pigments, cones respond to specific wavelengths of light. This allows color differentiation. The signal is transmitted to the bipolar cells and then to the ganglion cells. The visual signals from the retina are transmitted to the brain via the optic nerve. The neural pathway is as follows:

1. Optic Nerve: The ganglion cell axons form the optic nerve, which transmits signals from the retina to the brain.

2. Optic Chiasm: At the optic chiasm, the optic nerves from both eyes meet and partially cross. This allows visual information from the left field of vision (from both eyes) to be processed in the right hemisphere and vice versa.

3. Optic Tracts: After the chiasm, the visual signals travel along the optic tracts to the lateral geniculate nucleus (LGN) of the thalamus.

4. Lateral Geniculate Nucleus (LGN): The LGN acts as a relay station where visual signals are processed and sent to the visual cortex.

5. Primary Visual Cortex : Located in the occipital lobe, the V1 processes basic visual features such as orientation, contrast, and color.

6. Secondary Visual Areas :These areas process more complex visual information such as depth, motion, and object recognition.

Light entering the Eye

Six Steps to Vision

1. Light enters the eye through the cornea (clear, dome-shaped covering of the eye)

2. Then it passes through the pupil. The iris, or the colored part of your eye, controls the amount of light passing through.

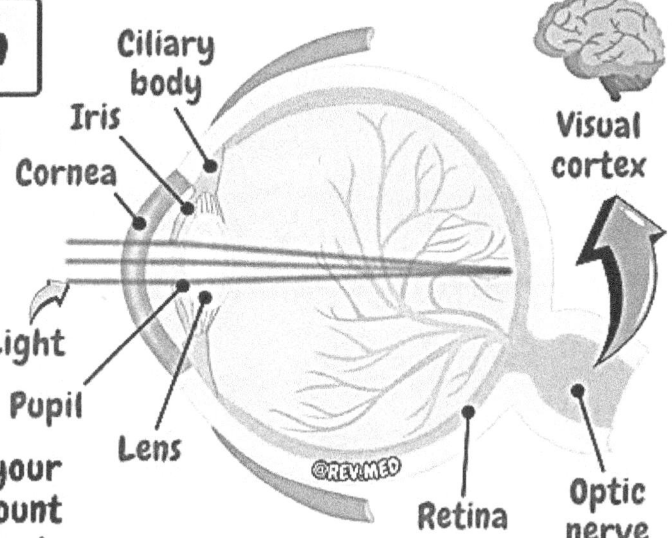

3. From there, it then hits the lens. This is the 'clear' structure inside the eye that focuses light rays onto the retina.

4. Next, light passes through the vitreous humor, clear, jelly-like substance that fills the center of the eye & keeps it round.

5. Finally, the light reaches the retina. This is the light-sensitive nerve layer that lines the back of the eye (contains photoreceptors: Rods & Cones). Here the image is inverted.

6. Optic nerve is then responsible for carrying chemical signals to the visual cortex of the brain. The visual cortex turns the signals into images (for example, our vision).

Visual Perception: How the Brain Interprets Visual Information

- Basic Visual Features:

  - **Color**: Perceived through the three types of cones (S, M, L) sensitive to different wavelengths.

  - **Shape and Size**: Processed by the visual cortex through complex integration of information.

  - **Depth**: Visual cues such as binocular disparity (difference in images from each eye) and monocular cues (relative size, motion parallax) help the brain perceive depth.

- Fusiform Face Area (FFA): Specializes in recognizing faces. This area is highly active when viewing faces, showing the brain's specialized processing for this visual category.

- Dorsal and Ventral Pathways:

  - **Dorsal Stream** ("Where" pathway): Processes spatial awareness and motion, helping the brain understand where objects are and how they are moving.

  - **Ventral Stream** ("What" pathway): Responsible for object recognition and identification.

Visual Disorders

Several visual disorders arise due to impairments in the structures or pathways involved in vision:

1. **Color Blindness**: Caused by defects in one or more types of cones, leading to the inability to perceive certain colors. It is typically inherited.

2. **Amblyopia (Lazy Eye)**: A condition where one eye does not develop normal vision, leading to reduced depth perception.

3. **Cataracts**: Clouding of the lens, which obstructs the passage of light to the retina.

4. **Glaucoma**: Damage to the optic nerve often due to high intraocular pressure, leading to vision loss.

5. **Macular Degeneration**: Degeneration of the central part of the retina (macula), leading to loss of central vision.

6. **Visual Agnosia**: An inability to recognize objects despite intact vision, typically resulting from damage to the ventral stream of the visual cortex.

7. The Psychological Aspect of Vision

- **Top-Down vs. Bottom-Up Processing**: Vision involves both bottom-up (sensory-driven) and top-down (knowledge-driven) processing.

  - **Bottom-Up**: The raw sensory data (light) is processed into recognizable patterns (e.g., edges, colors, and shapes).

  - **Top-Down**: Prior knowledge, expectations, and context influence how we interpret what we see (e.g., recognizing a face in a crowd).

- **Visual Illusions**: These demonstrate how the brain can be tricked into misinterpreting sensory input. For example, in the Müller-Lyer illusion, the brain perceives two lines of equal length as different lengths due to contextual cues.

Summary

Retina: Converts light into neural signals.

- **Photoreceptors**: Rods (low light) and cones (color, detail).

- **Optic Pathway**: From retina to occipital lobe.

- **Visual Processing**: The brain interprets visual stimuli through specialized areas for color, shape, depth, and motion.

- **Visual Disorders**: Various conditions can impair vision, from cataracts to neurological conditions like agnosia.

Auditory sense

The auditory system enables us to detect, interpret, and localize sound. It plays a vital role in communication, environmental awareness, learning, emotional regulation, and social development.

1. Nature of Sound

- Sound is a mechanical vibration that travels through a medium (usually air) in the form of pressure waves.
- Key properties:
- Frequency (Hz): Determines pitch.
- Amplitude (dB): Determines loudness.
- Timbre: The quality or texture of a sound, influenced by its harmonic structure.

2. Anatomy of the Auditory System

The auditory system is divided into three main sections: external ear, middle ear, and inner ear.

A. External Ear

- Pinna (Auricle): Captures and funnels sound waves into the ear canal.
- External Auditory Canal: Amplifies certain sound frequencies and directs sound waves to the tympanic membrane.
- Tympanic Membrane (Eardrum): Vibrates in response to sound waves.

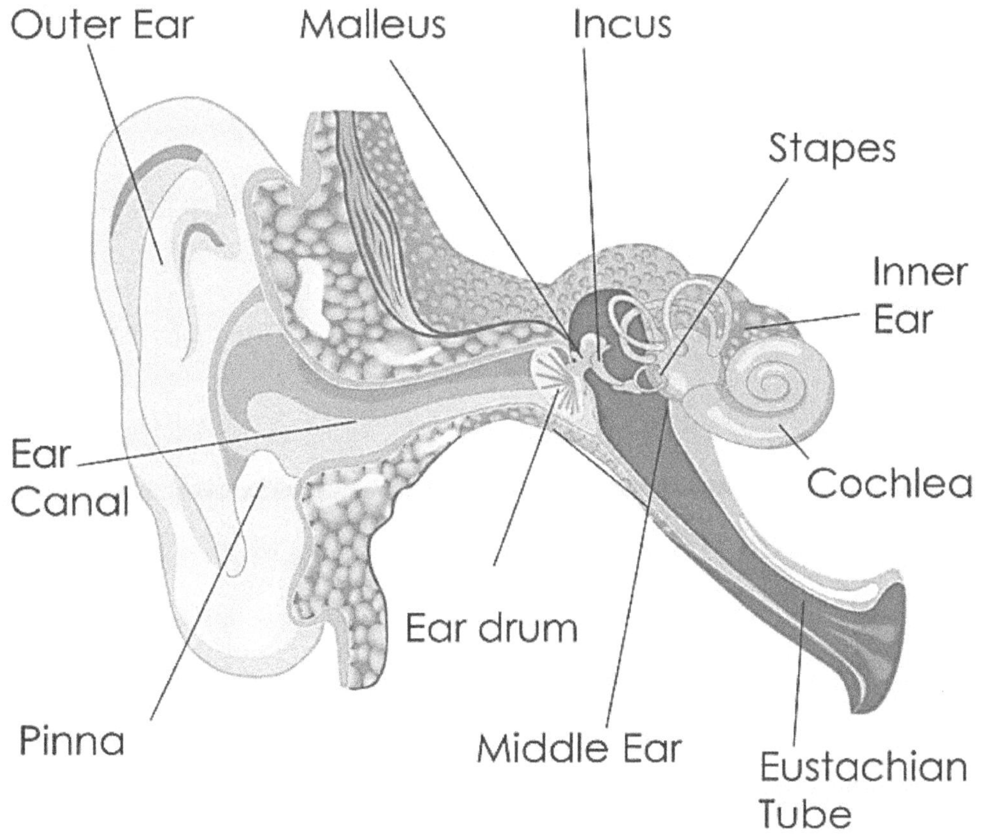

B. Middle Ear

- Contains three ossicles (smallest bones in the human body):

  - Malleus (hammer)

  - Incus (anvil)

  - Stapes (stirrup)

- These bones transmit and amplify vibrations from the tympanic membrane to the oval window of the inner ear.

  - Eustachian Tube: Connects the middle ear to the pharynx; equalizes pressure.

C. Inner Ear (Cochlea and Vestibular Apparatus)

- Cochlea:

- Spiral-shaped, fluid-filled structure responsible for converting mechanical vibrations into neural signals.

- Contains three chambers: scala vestibuli, scala media, and scala tympani.

- The scala media houses the Organ of Corti, the sensory receptor organ for hearing.

- Organ of Corti:

- Contains rows of inner and outer hair cells (mechanoreceptors).

- Sound-induced fluid movement in the cochlea deflects the basilar membrane, causing hair cells to bend against the tectorial membrane.

- Bending of hair cells opens ion channels, leading to neurotransmitter release and the initiation of nerve impulses.

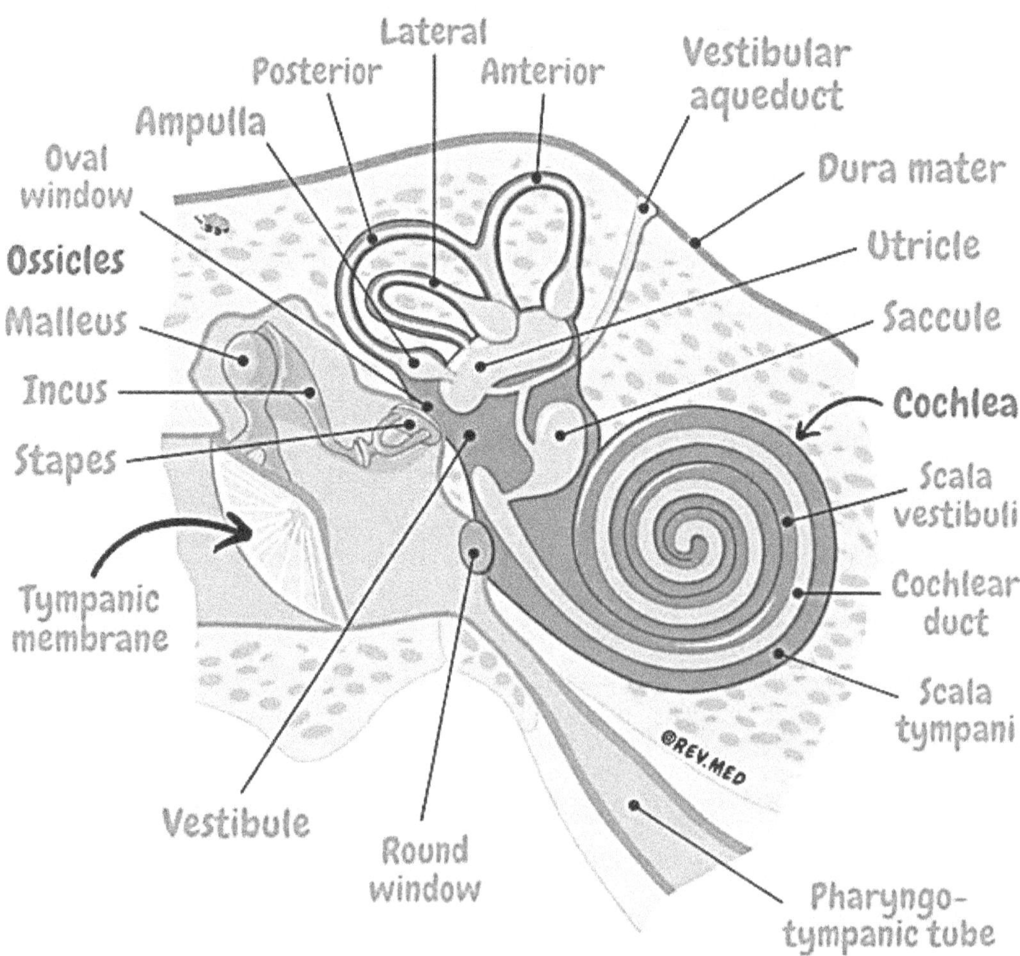

3. Neural Pathways of Audition

- Auditory Nerve (Cochlear Nerve): Carries impulses from the cochlea to the brainstem.
- Primary Auditory Pathway:

    1. Cochlear Nucleus (medulla)

    2. Superior Olivary Complex (pons): Involved in sound localization (binaural cues).

    3. Inferior Colliculus (midbrain): Integrates auditory reflexes.

    4. Medial Geniculate Nucleus (thalamus): Relays information to the cortex.

    5. Primary Auditory Cortex (Temporal Lobe; Heschl's gyrus): Final site of auditory perception (pitch, volume, tone, language comprehension).

- Secondary Auditory Cortex: Involved in complex auditory processing like speech, music, and language.
- Wernicke's Area (left hemisphere in most individuals): Interprets meaning of language.

4. Theories of Auditory Perception

A. Place Theory (Helmholtz)

- Proposes that different frequencies stimulate different places on the basilar membrane.

- High-frequency sounds affect the base of the cochlea; low frequencies affect the apex.

B. Frequency Theory

- Suggests that the frequency of auditory nerve firing corresponds to the frequency of the sound wave.

- Best explains low-frequency sound perception.

C. Volley Principle

- Combines frequency theory and place theory for intermediate frequencies.

- Groups of neurons fire in rapid succession to match the sound wave's frequency.

5. Psychophysical Concepts

- Absolute Threshold: Minimum intensity of sound detectable 50% of the time (~0 dB for healthy adults).
- Differential Threshold: Smallest difference between two sound frequencies a person can detect (just noticeable difference – JND).
- Masking: Presence of one sound makes another sound harder to hear (important in auditory attention and speech perception).

6. Disorders of the Auditory System

A. Conductive Hearing Loss

- Caused by damage to the outer or middle ear (e.g., otitis media, earwax blockage, ossicle dislocation).

- Sound waves are not efficiently conducted to the inner ear.

B. Sensorineural Hearing Loss

- Damage to the inner ear (cochlea) or auditory nerve.

- Causes: Aging (presbycusis), noise exposure, ototoxic drugs, infections, genetic factors.

C. Central Auditory Processing Disorder

- Dysfunction in the auditory pathways or cortex despite normal hearing sensitivity.

- Affects interpretation and processing of auditory information.

D. Tinnitus

- Perception of ringing or noise in the absence of external sound.

- Often linked to cochlear or auditory nerve damage.

7. Applications in Psychology and Therapy

- Counselling Implications:

- Hearing impairments can impact communication, emotional development, and social functioning.

- Audiological screening should be part of developmental, geriatric, and trauma-informed psychological assessments.

- Auditory Rehabilitation:

- Hearing aids and cochlear implants restore partial function.

- Auditory training and speech therapy help with processing and interpretation.

- Music Therapy and Sound Therapy:

- Used in anxiety, PTSD, emotional regulation, neurodevelopmental conditions (like autism).

- Exploits the brain's responsiveness to rhythm, melody, and vibration.

CONSCIOUSNESS AND STATES OF CONSCIOUSNESS

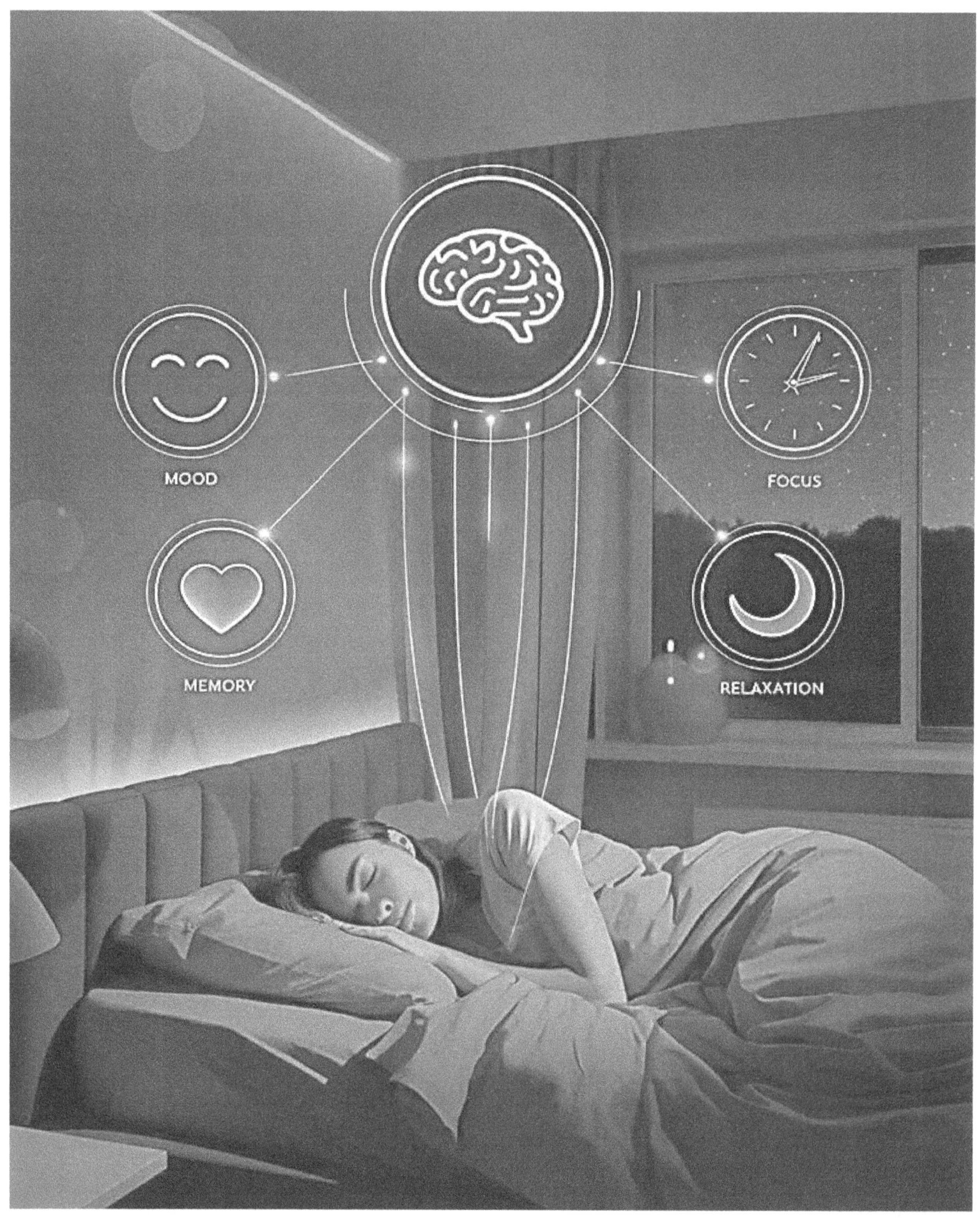

Sleep

Sleep: A natural altered state of consciousness

Ciccarelli and White define **sleep** as a: "Natural state of rest for the body and mind that involves a reversible loss of consciousness, characterized by distinct stages involving different levels of brain activity."

Sleep is **not simply the absence of wakefulness**, but an **active process** during which the brain is busy performing critical functions such as **healing, memory consolidation, and emotional processing**.

It is a **biologically regulated altered state of consciousness**, essential for both **physical restoration** and **psychological health**.

Biological Basis of Sleep

Sleep is **biologically driven** and controlled by the **brain and endocrine system**, regulated by **circadian rhythms and sleep pressure**.

A. Circadian Rhythms (The Body Clock)

- Governed by the **suprachiasmatic nucleus (SCN)** located in the **hypothalamus**.

- SCN is sensitive to **light signals** received by the retina.

- In darkness, SCN signals the **pineal gland** to release **melatonin**, which **induces sleep**.

- In light, melatonin production is suppressed, promoting **wakefulness**.

Disruptions to circadian rhythms (e.g., due to shift work or jet lag) can affect **mood, alertness, and health**.

B. Neurotransmitters and Hormones Involved

- **Melatonin**: Regulates sleep onset and circadian rhythms.

- **Serotonin**: Modulates sleep-wake transitions.

- **Adenosine**: Builds up during wakefulness, increasing sleep pressure.

- **GABA (Gamma-Aminobutyric Acid)**: Inhibitory neurotransmitter that promotes relaxation.

- **Acetylcholine**: Activates REM sleep.

Theories of sleep

Sleep is a universal biological behaviour, yet its exact purposes have been explored through various psychological and physiological lenses. Ciccarelli and White introduce several key **theories of sleep**, each emphasizing different aspects of its function: **restoration, adaptation, memory, and growth**.

1. Restorative Theory of Sleep

Sleep is necessary to **restore the body and mind**, allowing recovery from the wear and tear of daily functioning.

Biological Basis:

- During **deep (slow-wave) sleep**, the body:
    - Repairs **cell damage**.
    - Strengthens the **immune system**.
    - Releases **growth hormone**, particularly in children and adolescents.

Brain Functions:

- Sleep **clears out metabolic waste** from brain tissues (e.g., β-amyloid proteins linked with Alzheimer's).
- **Neurotransmitter levels** like serotonin and dopamine are replenished, which are crucial for mood regulation.

Psychological Relevance:

- After intense physical or mental activity, people tend to sleep **longer and more deeply**, supporting the restorative function.

2. Adaptive (Evolutionary) Theory of Sleep

Key Idea: Sleep evolved as a behaviour to **increase survival** by keeping organisms **inactive and hidden** during dangerous times.

Evolutionary Explanation:

- **Nocturnal rest** kept early humans and animals away from predators and environmental hazards at night.
- **Energy conservation**: By sleeping, energy is saved when activity is least efficient (e.g., at night without vision in humans).

Criticism:

- This theory doesn't fully explain **why the brain remains active during REM sleep**, or why sleep has restorative physiological effects.

3. Memory Consolidation Theory (Information-Processing Theory)

Key Idea: Sleep plays a critical role in **organizing, consolidating, and storing memories** from the day.

Cognitive Processes:

- During **REM sleep**, newly learned material and emotional experiences are consolidated.

- **NREM sleep**, especially stages 3 & 4, supports **declarative memory** (facts and knowledge).

- **REM sleep** supports **procedural memory** (skills and tasks) and **emotional processing**.

Research Support:

- Sleep deprivation impairs both **short-term and long-term memory**.

- Students perform better on tests after **a full night's sleep** than after sleep-deprived study.

4. Growth Theory (Hormonal/Developmental Theory)

Key Idea: Sleep is involved in **growth and brain development**, particularly in infancy and adolescence.

Endocrine Function:

- The **pituitary gland** releases **growth hormone (GH)** during **deep sleep**.

- This is essential for **physical development and repair**.

In Children:

- Infants spend **more time in REM sleep**, which supports **neural plasticity and brain maturation**.

5. Brain Plasticity and Learning Theory

Key Idea: Sleep is necessary for **restructuring neural connections**, a process essential for **learning and adapting**.

Neural Networks:

- During sleep, especially REM, the brain **reorganizes synaptic connections** based on what was learned during wakefulness.

- Encourages **neuroplasticity**, which is essential for psychological adaptation and mental health.

Neurocognitive Findings:

- Functional MRI studies show **hippocampal activity** during sleep reflects recent memory encoding.

- Sleep enhances **insight and creative problem-solving**.

6. Clean-up Theory (Glymphatic System Theory)

Emerging Neuroscience-Based Theory

Key Idea: Sleep helps the brain **remove waste and toxins** via the glymphatic system.

Glymphatic Flow:

- During sleep, especially NREM, the **interstitial spaces between neurons expand**, allowing the brain to **flush out neurotoxins**.

- This helps prevent **neurodegenerative disorders** like Alzheimer's.

Summary:

Theory	Focus	Key Functions
Restorative Theory	Biological repair	Tissue repair, neurotransmitter restoration, immune strengthening
Adaptive Theory	Evolution & survival	Inactivity during dangerous periods, energy conservation
Memory Consolidation	Cognitive processing	Consolidates learning, enhances memory, emotional regulation
Growth Theory	Hormonal and developmental processes	Growth hormone release, brain maturation in children
Brain Plasticity Theory	Neural adaptability	Rewiring neural circuits, learning enhancement
Clean-Up (Glymphatic) Theory	Waste removal via CSF	Detoxification, prevention of brain diseases

Sleep deprivation

Sleep deprivation refers to the **condition of not getting sufficient sleep**, either in terms of **duration** or **quality**, to support optimal physical, emotional, and cognitive functioning.

sleep deprivation occurs when a person gets **significantly less sleep than needed**, which can severely impair **concentration, memory, coordination, emotional regulation**, and overall **health**.

Types of Sleep Deprivation

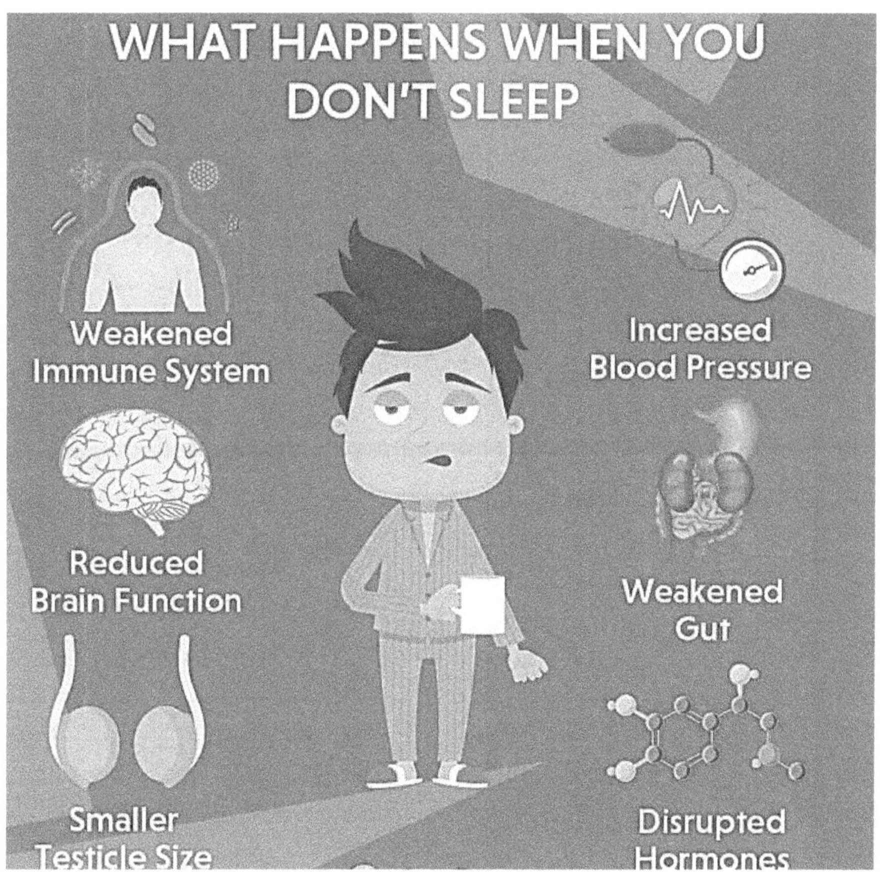

Type	Description
Acute Sleep Deprivation	Short-term lack of sleep (e.g., staying up all night before an exam).
Chronic Sleep Deprivation	Long-term sleep loss (e.g., regularly sleeping less than 5–6 hours per night).
Partial Sleep Deprivation	Getting some sleep but less than needed over consecutive days.
Total Sleep Deprivation	No sleep at all over an extended period (usually 24+ hours).

Causes of Sleep Deprivation

- **Lifestyle factors** (late-night screen use, poor sleep hygiene)

- **Work schedules** (shift work, long hours, night duties)

- **Academic stress**

- **Mental health issues** (e.g., anxiety, depression, PTSD)

- **Medical conditions** (e.g., sleep apnea, chronic pain)

- **Substance use** (e.g., caffeine, stimulants, alcohol)

- **Technology overuse** (blue light inhibits melatonin production)

Psychological and Cognitive Effects

Sleep deprivation has **profound effects on the brain and behaviour**, many of which have been studied through **EEG, neuroimaging, and cognitive performance tasks**.

Cognitive Impairments:

- **Poor attention and concentration**

- **Slower reaction times**

- **Impaired decision-making and problem-solving**

- **Decreased working memory**

- **Reduced learning and retention**

Sleep loss particularly affects the **prefrontal cortex**, the area responsible for **executive functions** like planning, impulse control, and reasoning.

5. Emotional and Behavioural Consequences

- **Mood swings** (irritability, frustration)

- **Increased risk of anxiety and depression**

- **Reduced stress tolerance**

- **Emotional dysregulation** (e.g., overreacting to small events)

- **Social withdrawal and interpersonal conflict**

Sleep-deprived individuals often have heightened activity in the **amygdala** (emotion-processing center), resulting in **exaggerated emotional responses**.

6. Physical and Biological Effects

- **Weakened immune system**

- **Increased inflammation**

- **Hormonal imbalances** (e.g., increased cortisol, reduced growth hormone)

- **Risk of obesity** (due to hormonal shifts: $\downarrow$ leptin, $\uparrow$ ghrelin)

- **Increased risk for cardiovascular issues** (e.g., high blood pressure)

- **Microsleeps** – brief, uncontrollable episodes of sleep lasting a few seconds

7. Impact on Learning and Memory

Ciccarelli and White emphasize the **critical role of sleep in memory consolidation**. Lack of sleep:

- Impairs **declarative memory** (facts, knowledge)

- Disrupts **procedural memory** (skills, routines)

- Weakens **emotional memory processing**

- Reduces **neuroplasticity**, making new learning difficult

8. Sleep Deprivation and Mental Health

Key Connections:

- Increases vulnerability to **mood disorders**

- Worsens symptoms of **depression and anxiety**

- Can trigger **mania** in individuals with bipolar disorder

- Associated with **psychotic-like symptoms** in extreme cases (e.g., hallucinations, paranoia)

9. Sleep Debt and Recovery Sleep

- **Sleep debt** is the **cumulative effect of not getting enough sleep**, resulting in a strong **drive for rebound sleep**.

- Recovery sleep can help reverse some effects (especially cognitive), but **chronic deprivation has long-term consequences** that can't be fully reversed with a few nights of good rest.

10. Sleep Deprivation in Real-Life Contexts

Population	Consequences
Students	Poor academic performance, memory issues, emotional instability
Healthcare Workers	Medical errors, burnout, impaired judgment
Shift Workers	Disrupted circadian rhythms, increased risk of metabolic disorders
Drivers	Increased accident risk (similar to being legally intoxicated)

Summary:

Domain Affected	Effects of Sleep Deprivation
Cognitive	↓ Attention, ↓ Memory, ↓ Learning, ↓ Decision-making
Emotional	↑ Anxiety, ↑ Irritability, ↓ Emotional regulation
Physical	↓ Immunity, ↑ Cortisol, ↑ Blood pressure, ↑ Risk of obesity
Social	Poor communication, Social withdrawal, Interpersonal conflict
Mental Health	↑ Risk of depression, mania, hallucinations (in extreme deprivation)

How to Get
Good Sleep
When Seasons Change
1 Stick to a schedule
Keep a consistent sleep-wake-up routine
2 Start the day with sunlight
Light helps you wake up & prevent grogginess
3 Get moving & grooving
Daily exercise can help you fall asleep more quickly
4 Relieve stress before bed
Journaling, meditation & yoga can help you relax
5 Set the mood
Keep your room cool, dark & quiet to prevent sleep disruptors
6 Avoid late-night meals
Eat at least 3 hours before bedtime
7 Nix the nightcaps
Drinking can make it harder to fall asleep & stay asleep
8 Stop the scrolling
Blue light before bed can keep your brain wired

12 Tips For Healthy Sleep
Stick to a sleep schedule
Exercise is great, but not too late in the day
Avoid caffeine and nicotine
Avoid alcoholic drinks before bed
Avoid large meals and beverages late at night
If possible, avoid medicines that delay or disrupt your sleep
Don't take naps after 3 p.m.
Relax before bed
Take a hot bath before bed
Have a dark bedroom, cool bedroom, gadget-free bedroom
Have the right sunlight exposure
Don't lie in bed awake

Strategies for Good Sleep Hygiene:

- Maintain a **consistent sleep schedule**

- Avoid screens before bedtime

- Limit caffeine and alcohol intake

- Create a **quiet, dark, and cool sleeping environment**

- Practice **relaxation techniques** (e.g., deep breathing, meditation)

- Seek professional help for **sleep disorders**

Stages of Sleep: NREM and REM

Sleep is not a single uniform state but a **dynamic, cyclic process** that alternates between different stages of **NREM (Non-Rapid Eye Movement)** and **REM (Rapid Eye Movement)** sleep. These stages are **cyclical**, typically repeating **every 90–110 minutes** throughout the night.

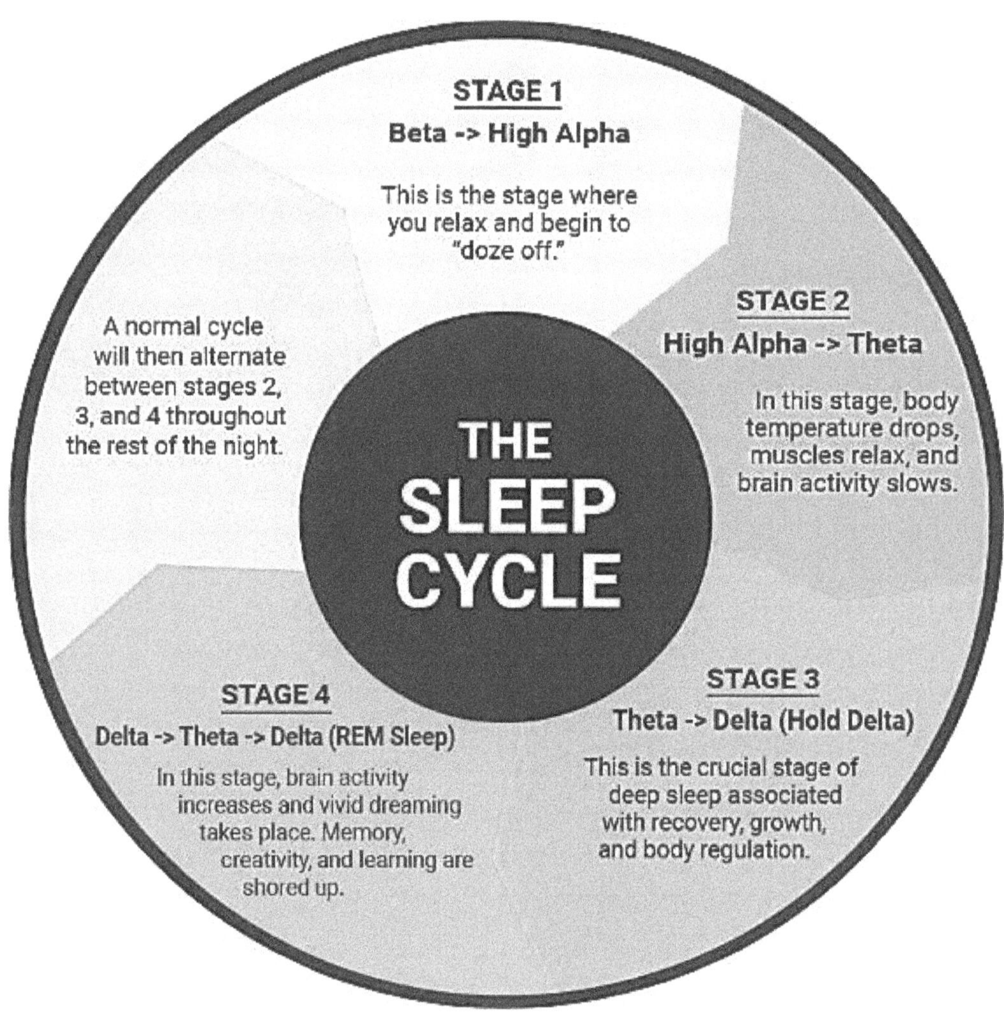

Type of Sleep	
NREM Sleep	Non-dreaming sleep; body is relaxed; crucial for physical recovery and memory.
REM Sleep	Active dreaming state; brain is highly active; body is immobile (muscle atonia).

Sleep Cycle

- A healthy adult passes through **4–6 sleep cycles per night**.

- Each cycle progresses through **NREM stages (1–3)** and ends in **REM**.

- As the night progresses:

○ **REM periods get longer**, and

○ **Deep NREM sleep (stage 3) gets shorter**.

NREM Sleep Stages (Stages 1–3)

Stage 1 (N1): Light Sleep

- **Transition from wakefulness to sleep**

- Lasts a few minutes (5–10 mins)

- **Brain waves:** Theta waves begin to appear

- **Features:**

○ Muscle activity slows down

○ Hypnic jerks or sudden muscle contractions may occur

○ May experience **hypnagogic hallucinations** (brief dreamlike images)

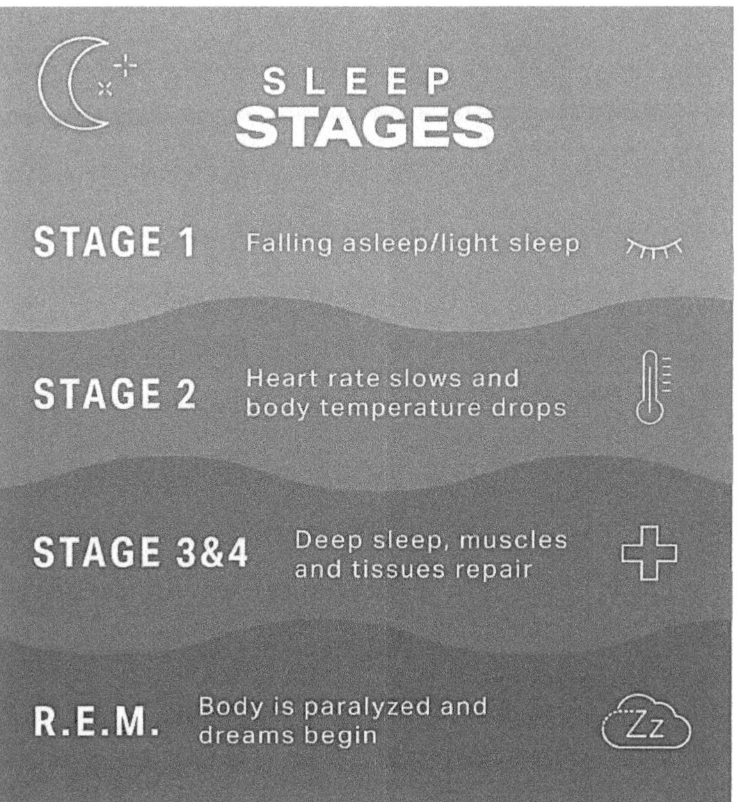

Ciccarelli notes this as a **"drifting" state** where people may not even realize they were asleep.

Stage 2 (N2): Moderate Sleep

- Lasts 10–25 minutes in the first cycle; longer in later cycles

- **Brain waves:** Sleep spindles (bursts of brain activity) and K-complexes

- Body temperature drops, heart rate slows

- **Conscious awareness disappears**

Sleep spindles are linked to **memory consolidation** and **sensory processing**.

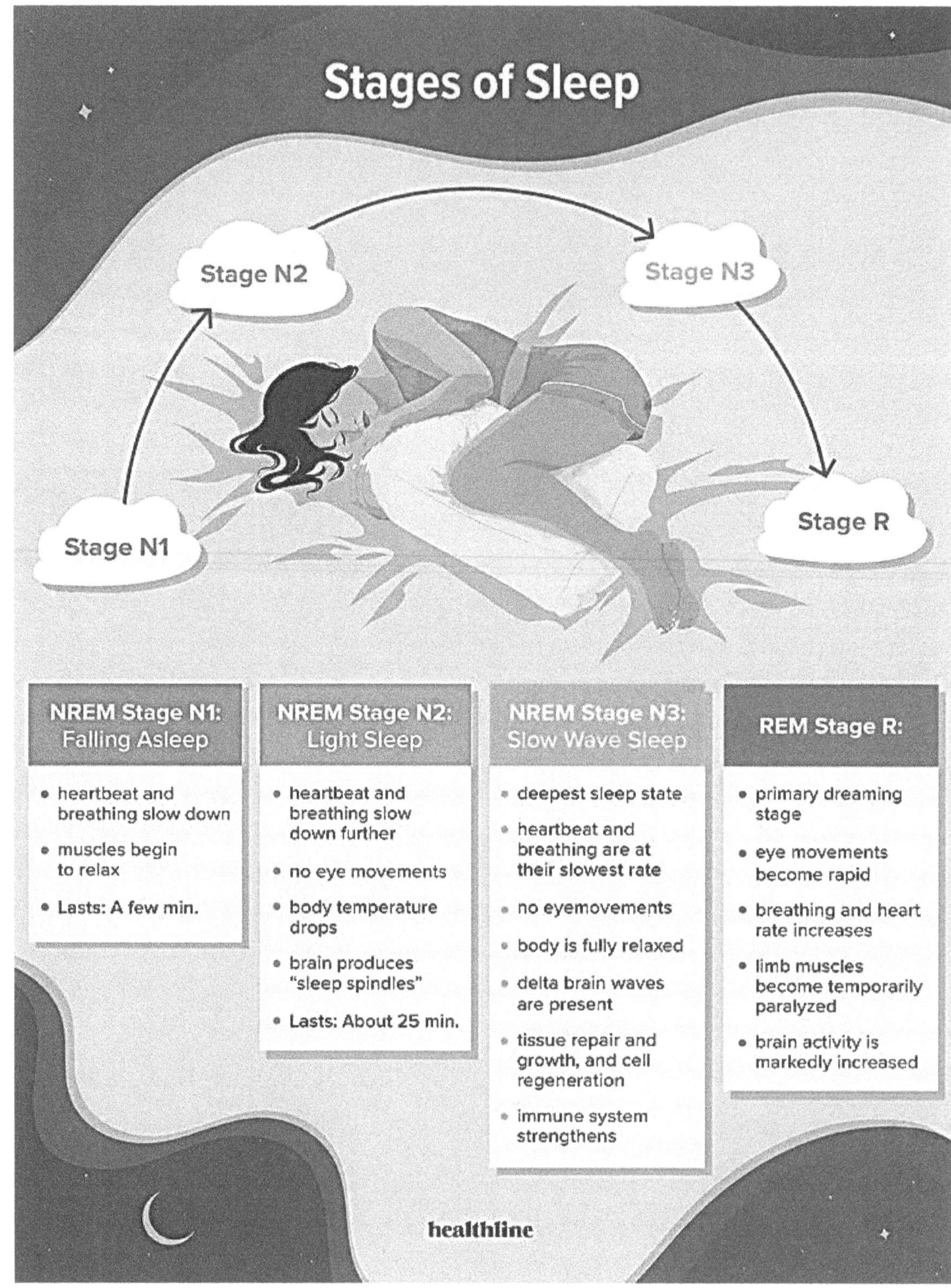

Stage 3 (N3): Deep Sleep / Slow-Wave Sleep (SWS)

- Also known as **Delta Sleep**
- **Brain waves:** Large, slow **delta waves**
- Very hard to wake someone in this stage
- **Body repairs itself**: hormone release (e.g., growth hormone), immune functioning
- Important for **physical restoration and memory consolidation**

Ciccarelli emphasizes this as the most **restorative stage** of sleep, critical for feeling refreshed.

REM Sleep: Rapid Eye Movement Sleep

Stage 4: REM Sleep

- Occurs about **90 minutes after falling asleep**
- **Brain waves resemble wakefulness**: fast, low-voltage beta-like waves
- **Dreams are vivid and emotional**
- Body is in **paralysis (muscle atonia)** to prevent acting out dreams
- Eyes move rapidly under closed eyelids

Features of REM:

Feature	Description
Dreaming	80–90% of vivid dreams occur in REM
Paradoxical sleep	Brain is active, but the body is immobile
Memory consolidation	Especially important for **emotional and procedural memories**
Brain activity	Increased activity in **amygdala, hippocampus, and visual association areas**

REM sleep enhances brain plasticity, creativity, and emotional balance.

Sleep Cycle Progression (Simplified)

Typical Sleep Cycle:
N1 → N2 → N3 → N2 → REM → (Repeat)

- First few cycles: more **N3 (deep sleep)**
- Later cycles: longer **REM periods**

Comparison: NREM vs REM

Feature	NREM Sleep (Stages 1–3)	REM Sleep
Brain Waves	Theta → Delta (slow waves)	Fast, irregular (similar to waking)
Dreaming	Rare or vague dreams	Vivid, story-like dreams
Body Activity	Some movement possible	Paralysis (muscle atonia)
Functions	Physical repair, memory, immune functioning	Memory, emotional regulation, learning
Sleep Onset	Begins with NREM	Follows after ~90 minutes of sleep
Importance	Vital for **physical** restoration	Vital for **psychological** restoration

Clinical Relevance

- Disruptions in NREM sleep are associated with **fatigue**, **immune dysfunction**, and **pain sensitivity**.

- Disrupted REM sleep is linked to:

    - **Depression and anxiety**

    - **Impaired emotional regulation**

    - **PTSD-related nightmares**

Purpose of REM Sleep

REM (Rapid Eye Movement) sleep isn't just for vivid dreaming—it's *crucial for psychological, cognitive, and neural health*. Here's a breakdown of its purposes.

1. Cognitive Restoration and Brain Plasticity

- REM sleep enhances **neural connectivity** and **synaptic pruning** (removal of unnecessary neural connections).

- Facilitates **learning and memory consolidation**, especially for **procedural** and **emotional memories** (e.g., riding a bike, social skills, emotional coping).

2. Emotional Regulation

- REM sleep processes **emotional experiences**, helping regulate moods and reduce emotional reactivity.

- Reduced REM has been linked with **irritability**, **anxiety**, and even **depressive symptoms**.

3. Dreaming and Psychological Processing

- Dreams during REM allow the **brain to simulate and process complex emotions**, conflicts, or scenarios.
- May serve a **"safe rehearsal" function**, helping us mentally navigate social and survival challenges.

4. Cognitive Development

- Infants spend up to **50% of sleep in REM**, suggesting a strong link with **brain maturation and development**.
- Adults average ~20–25% REM sleep, still vital for ongoing mental flexibility and memory.

REM Rebound: What Happens When REM is Deprived?

REM Rebound is the **intensified and extended REM sleep** that occurs after a period of **REM deprivation** (e.g., due to stress, alcohol, certain medications, or all-nighters).

Features of REM Rebound:

Effect	Explanation
Increased REM duration	The brain compensates by entering REM sleep **faster** and staying in it **longer**
More intense dreams	Often vivid, bizarre, and emotionally charged dreams may occur

Heightened physiological activity	Increased heart rate, eye movements, and brain activation

It Happens because:

- The body **prioritizes REM sleep** because it's **essential for mental health** and memory.

- REM deprivation **disrupts emotional equilibrium**, so the brain "catches up" aggressively when allowed to recover.

Sleep Disorders

Disorders that **interfere with the normal pattern of sleep** and significantly impact physical and psychological health.

Ciccarelli & White categorize sleep disorders under **two broad types**:

1. Dyssomnias – Disorders related to the amount, quality, or timing of sleep

2. Parasomnias – Involve abnormal behaviours or experiences during sleep

1. Dyssomnias

These disorders involve **problems in the sleep-wake cycle**—difficulty falling asleep, staying asleep, or excessive sleepiness.

a) Insomnia

- **Definition**: Persistent difficulty in falling asleep, staying asleep, or getting quality sleep

- **Causes**: Stress, anxiety, depression, irregular routines, poor sleep hygiene

- **Effects**:
  - Daytime fatigue
  - Irritability and poor concentration
  - Increased risk of depression and anxiety

- Insomnia is the **most common sleep disorder**, and often **stress-related** or **behaviourally maintained** (e.g., bad sleep habits).

b) Sleep Apnea

- **Definition**: A person **stops breathing for 10 seconds or more** during sleep—often multiple times per night

  o **Obstructive sleep apnea (OSA)**: Blockage of the airway

  o **Central sleep apnea**: Brain fails to signal breathing

- **Symptoms**:

  o Loud snoring

  o Choking/gasping during sleep

  o Daytime drowsiness

- **Risks**: Heart disease, high blood pressure, cognitive issues

- **Treatment**: CPAP machine, weight loss, surgery

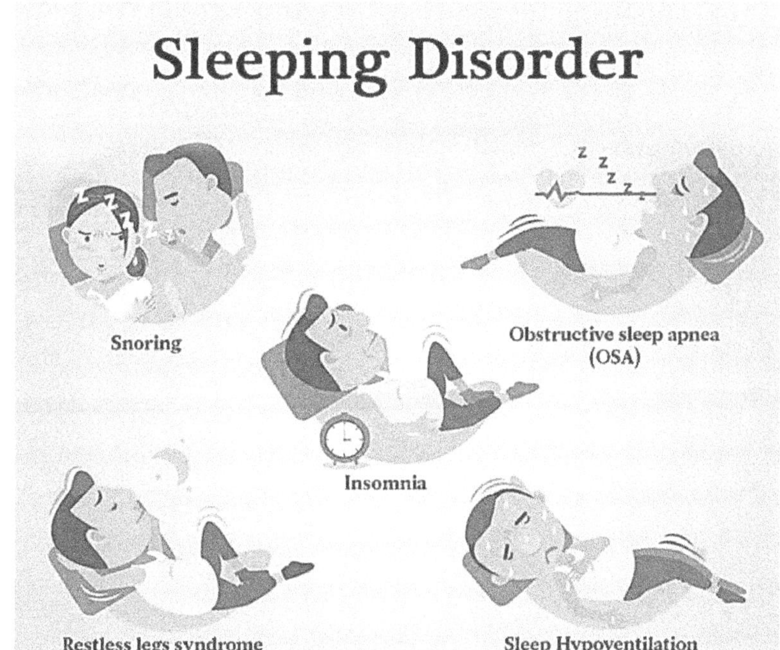

sleep apnea is **highly underdiagnosed** but very **disruptive to deep (N3) sleep and REM**, causing fatigue even after "sleeping" for hours.

c) Narcolepsy

- A **chronic neurological disorder** where the brain **suddenly switches into REM sleep**, even during waking hours

- **Symptoms**:

  o Sudden **"sleep attacks"**

  o **Cataplexy** (sudden loss of muscle tone)

  o Hallucinations at sleep onset or waking

- **Cause**: Genetic; associated with hypocretin/orexin deficiency in the hypothalamus

- **Impact**: Dangerous during activities like driving or walking

- **Treatment**: Medication, scheduled naps, sleep hygiene

Ciccarelli describes it as a **"REM intrusion disorder"**, where the **boundaries between sleep and wake blur**.

d) Restless Leg Syndrome (RLS)

RLS is a **neurological sensory-motor disorder** where a person experiences **uncomfortable sensations in the legs** (sometimes arms) and an **urge to move them**, especially during rest or inactivity, mostly in the evening or at night.

Symptoms:

- Tingling, itching, crawling, pulling sensations

- Temporary relief when legs are moved or stretched

- Symptoms worsen at night and **disrupt falling asleep**

- Can result in **insomnia** or **fragmented sleep**

Causes & Associations:

- Often **idiopathic**, but can be associated with:

  - **Iron deficiency**

  - **Peripheral neuropathy**

  - **Pregnancy**

  - **Parkinson's disease**

- May have a **genetic component**

2. Parasomnias

These involve **unusual behaviours** during sleep, mostly during **deep NREM (stage 3)** sleep or transitions between stages.

a) Sleepwalking (Somnambulism)

- Occurs in **N3 deep sleep** (not REM!)

- **Complex behaviours** (walking, dressing, even eating) without conscious awareness

- More common in children

- Person may appear awake but is **not responsive**

- **Myth busted**: It is not dangerous to wake a sleepwalker, but they may be disoriented

b) Night Terrors (Sleep Terrors)

- Occur during **N3** (not REM)

- Sudden arousal with **screaming, panic, rapid heartbeat**

- The person **does not remember** the episode

- Common in children; linked to **overarousal of CNS**

- Unlike nightmares, they occur in **non-dreaming sleep**

Ciccarelli explains night terrors as **biologically driven arousals**, separate from emotional dreaming.

c) REM Sleep Behaviour Disorder (RBD)

- Involves **acting out dreams** due to **lack of muscle paralysis (atonia)** in REM

- Movements can be violent or dangerous

- More common in **older adults** and may be linked to **neurodegenerative disorders** like Parkinson's

- Often requires **medication** and **safety measures** (e.g., padded surroundings)

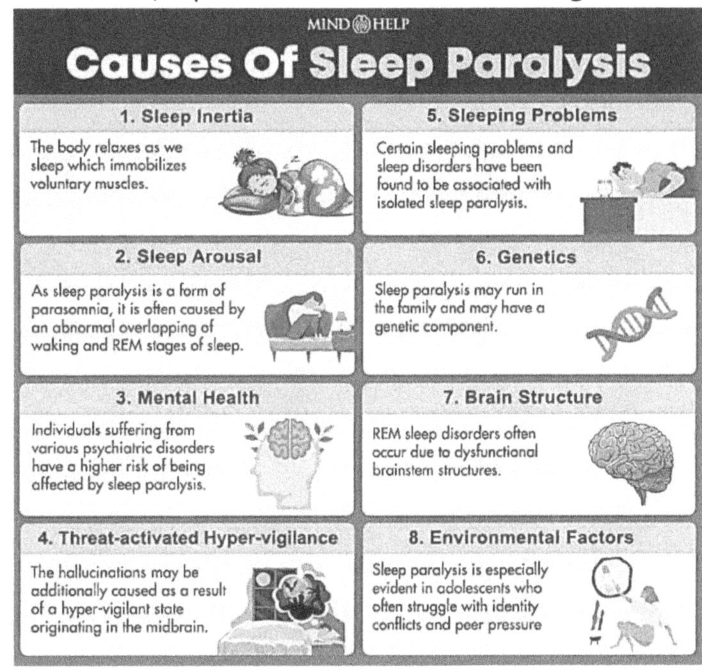

d) Nightmares

- Vivid, disturbing dreams that **occur in REM sleep**

- Person usually **wakes up and remembers** the content

- Triggered by stress, trauma, or anxiety

- Unlike night terrors, the person is **aware and can recall the dream**

Ciccarelli points out that **frequent nightmares** can be symptoms of **PTSD or generalized anxiety**.

e) Sleep Paralysis

It is a **temporary inability to move or speak** while **falling asleep (hypnagogic)** or **waking up (hypnopompic)**. The person is *conscious* but **cannot move**, which can feel frightening.

- Occurs during the transition between **wakefulness and REM sleep**.

- The **body is in REM atonia (paralyzed)**, but the **mind becomes awake**.

- Often accompanied by:

o A sense of pressure on the chest

o Hallucinations (visual, auditory, or tactile)

○ Intense fear or a feeling of a "presence" in the room

- Episodes usually last from a **few seconds to a couple of minutes**.

Causes:

- **Sleep deprivation**

- **Irregular sleep schedule**

- **High stress**

- **Narcolepsy** (Sleep paralysis can be a symptom)

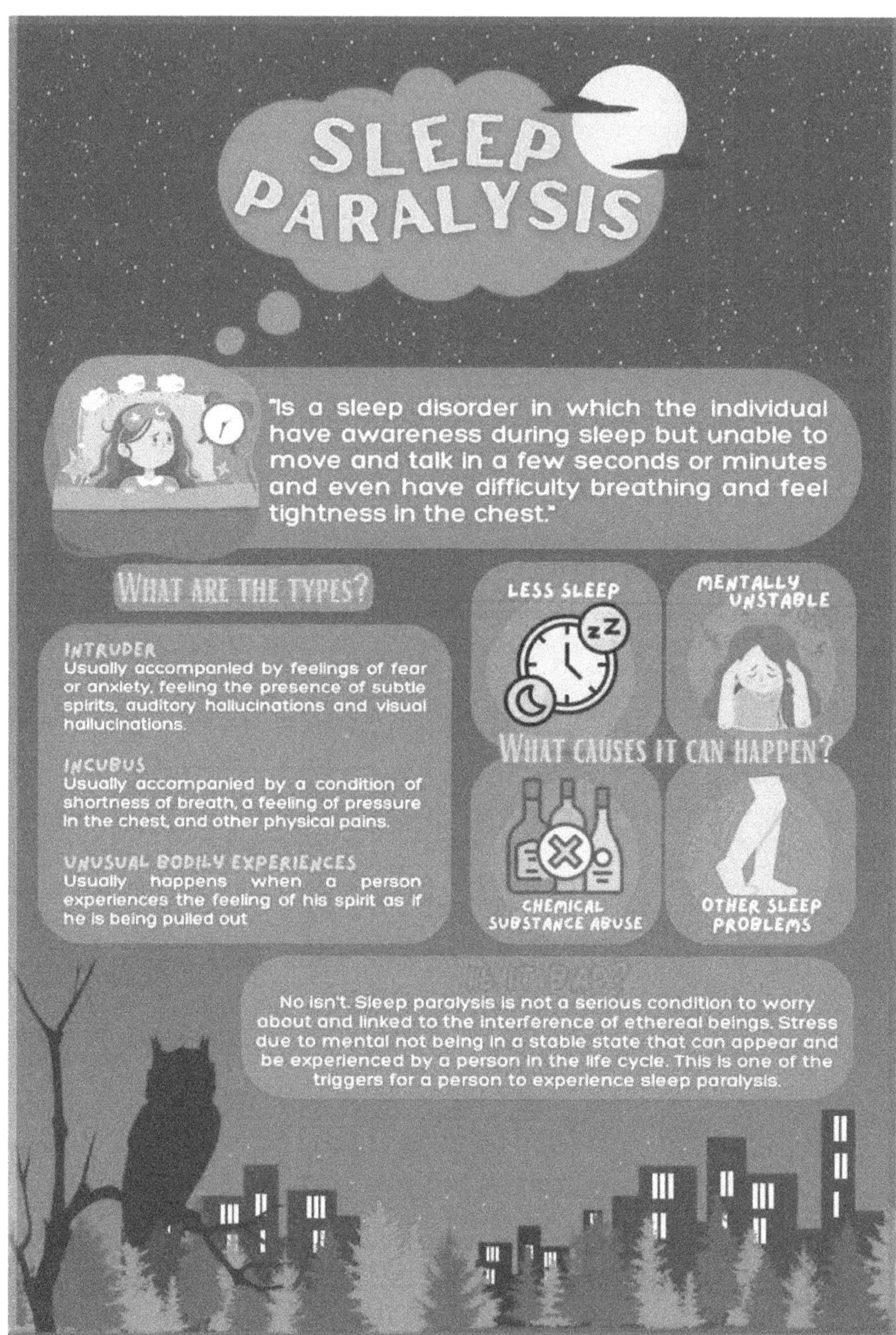

Quick Recap: Common Sleep Disorders

Disorder	Type	Key Feature	Sleep Stage Affected
Insomnia	Dyssomnia	Trouble falling/staying asleep	All stages
Sleep Apnea	Dyssomnia	Repeated breathing pauses	NREM + REM
Narcolepsy	Dyssomnia	Sudden REM sleep intrusions	Wake to REM transition
Sleepwalking	Parasomnia	Complex actions during sleep	N3 (Deep NREM)
Night Terrors	Parasomnia	Screaming/panic without memory	N3 (Deep NREM)
Nightmares	Parasomnia	Disturbing dreams, person remembers	REM
REM Sleep Behaviour Disorder	Parasomnia	Physically acting out vivid dreams	REM

MEMORY, LEARNING AND EMOTION

Memory

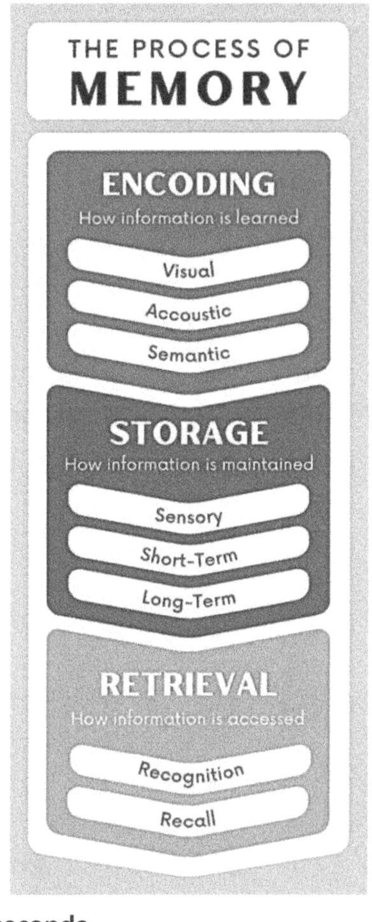

Memory is the **cognitive and physiological process** by which the brain encodes, stores, and retrieves information. It allows organisms to retain past experiences and use this information in the present or future.

- **Encoding**: The process of converting sensory input into a form that can be stored in the brain.

- **Storage**: The process of maintaining information over time.

- **Retrieval**: Accessing stored information when needed.

Types of Memory

A. Sensory Memory

This is the **briefest form** of memory. It holds **sensory information** for a few milliseconds to a few seconds.

- **Iconic Memory** (Visual): Stores visual information (images, scenes) for about **0.5–1 second**.

- **Echoic Memory** (Auditory): Stores sound-based information for about **2–4 seconds**.

Example: When you glance at something quickly, the image lingers momentarily even after you close your eyes.

Sensory memory acts as a buffer for stimuli received through the senses and feeds information to short-term memory if attended to.

B. Short-Term Memory (STM) / Working Memory

- Holds a small amount of information (about **7 ± 2 items**) for a short duration (**15–30 seconds**).

- If not rehearsed, the information is lost.

Working Memory refers to:

- The ability to **hold and manipulate** information in real-time.

- **Baddeley's Model** includes:

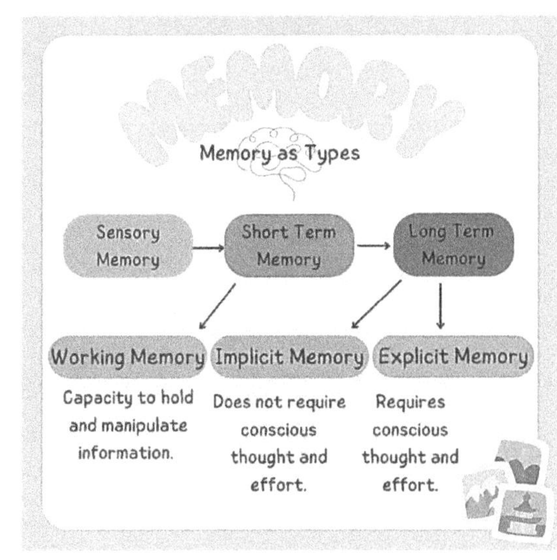

- ○ **Central Executive** – controls attention

- ○ **Phonological Loop** – auditory information

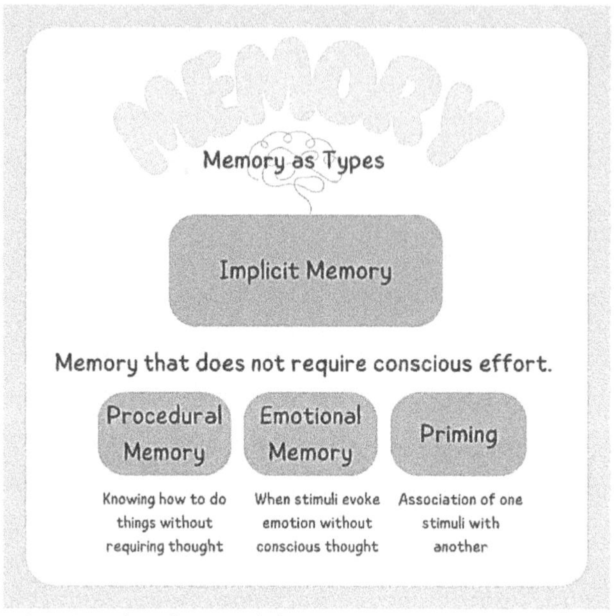

- ○ **Visuospatial Sketchpad** – visual and spatial data

- ○ **Episodic Buffer** – integrates information across domains

  Example: Mentally solving a math problem or remembering a phone number temporarily.

C. Long-Term Memory (LTM)

Stores information for a **long duration**, potentially a lifetime. It has **unlimited capacity**. It is subdivided into:

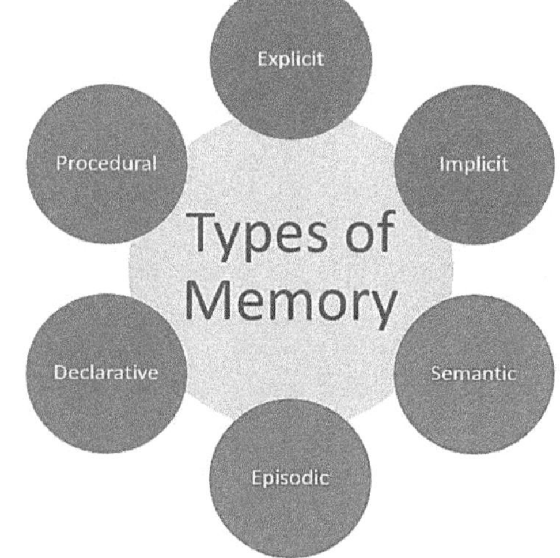

1. Declarative (Explicit) Memory

- Conscious recall of facts and events.

- Depends heavily on the **hippocampus and medial temporal lobe**.

Types:

- **Episodic Memory**: Personal experiences and autobiographical events.

    - ○ *Example*: Your last birthday celebration.

- **Semantic Memory**: General world knowledge, concepts, language.

    - ○ *Example*: Knowing that Paris is the capital of France.

2. Non-declarative (Implicit) Memory

- Unconscious, automatic memory that influences thoughts or behaviours without conscious awareness.

- Involves **subcortical structures** like the **cerebellum and basal ganglia**.

Types:

- **Procedural Memory**: Skills and actions.

    o *Example*: Riding a bicycle, typing on a keyboard.

- **Priming**: Previous exposure to a stimulus influences future responses.

    o *Example*: Seeing the word "yellow" might make you quicker to recognize the word "banana."

- **Classical Conditioning**: Learned responses to stimuli.

    o *Example*: Salivating at the sound of a bell if it has been repeatedly paired with food.

Summary

Memory Type	Duration	Conscious?	Brain Areas Involved	Example
Sensory	0.5–4 sec	No	Sensory cortices	Glance at an image
Short-Term	15–30 sec	Yes	Prefrontal cortex	Holding a phone number
Working	Active use	Yes	Prefrontal cortex, parietal lobe	Doing mental math
Long-Term	Unlimited	Yes/No	Hippocampus, cortex, cerebellum	Learning to drive
→ **Declarative**	Long-lasting	Yes	Hippocampus, neocortex	Recalling a birthday
→ **Implicit**	Long-lasting	No	Cerebellum, basal ganglia	Tying your shoes

3. Neural Structures Involved in Memory

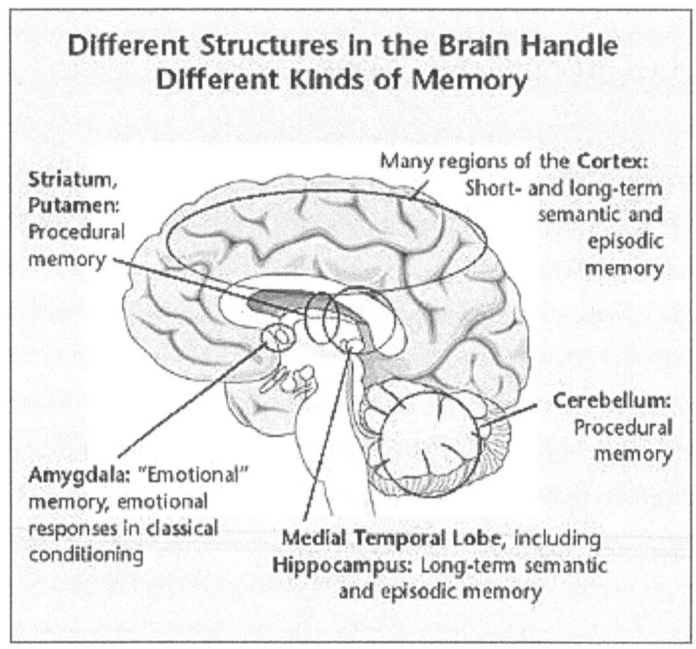

1. Hippocampus

- *Location*: Medial temporal lobe.

- *Function*:

  o Essential for the **formation, organization, and consolidation of new long-term declarative memories** (facts and personal experiences).

  o Transfers information from **short-term memory to long-term memory**.

- *Case Study*:

  o **HM (Henry Molaison)**: After removal of his hippocampi, he couldn't form new declarative memories (anterograde amnesia), proving the hippocampus is vital for memory consolidation.

- Damage results in:

  o Anterograde amnesia.

  o Difficulty in spatial navigation (e.g., getting lost).

2. Amygdala

- *Location*: Deep within the temporal lobe, adjacent to the hippocampus.
- *Function*:
    - o Involved in **emotional aspects of memory**, especially **fear-related learning**.
    - o Helps tag emotional significance to memories, making emotional memories stronger and easier to recall.
- Interaction:
    - o Works closely with the hippocampus to strengthen emotional memories.
- Damage can lead to:
    - o Poor fear conditioning and inability to recognize emotional significance of events.

3. Prefrontal Cortex (PFC)

- *Location*: Frontal lobe, just behind the forehead.
- *Function*:
    - o Controls **working memory** – temporary storage and manipulation of information (e.g., mental math).
    - o Involved in **executive functions** like planning, attention, and decision-making.
    - o Helps organize and retrieve stored memories.
- *Example*:
    - o Remembering a phone number briefly before dialing.
- Damage leads to:
    - o Disorganized thinking, poor memory retrieval, and difficulty holding attention.

4. Cerebellum

- *Location*: Back of the brain, under the occipital lobes.
- *Function*:
    - o Encodes **procedural memory** (e.g., skills like riding a bicycle, typing).
    - o Coordinates **motor learning** and fine-tunes movement.
- Part of implicit memory system – does not require conscious recall.
- Damage results in:

- o   Poor motor coordination and impaired learning of motor skills.

5. Basal Ganglia

- *Location*: Deep within cerebral hemispheres.
- *Function*:
    - o   Supports **habit formation**, **automatic behaviours**, and **procedural learning**.
    - o   Involved in learning routines and sequences (e.g., tying shoelaces, driving).
- Works with cerebellum and cortex to refine motor actions.
- Damage linked to:
    - o   Parkinson's disease (affecting movement and motor memory).

6. Thalamus & Mammillary Bodies

- *Location*: Deep midbrain structures, part of the limbic system.
- *Function*:
    - o   **Thalamus**: Acts as a relay station for sensory and motor signals; plays a role in attention and filtering relevant memory inputs.
    - o   **Mammillary Bodies**: Associated with recollective memory; part of the **Papez Circuit** – a memory loop crucial for declarative memory and emotional expression.
- *Clinical Relevance*:
    - o   Damage seen in **Korsakoff's syndrome** (often due to chronic alcoholism and vitamin B1 deficiency), leading to severe memory loss and confabulation.

Summary

Brain Structure	Memory Role	Damage Results In
Hippocampus	Forms new long-term declarative memories	Anterograde amnesia
Amygdala	Emotional tagging of memories	Impaired emotional learning
Prefrontal Cortex	Working memory, attention, decision-making	Disorganized thinking
Cerebellum	Procedural/motor memory	Poor motor learning
Basal Ganglia	Habits, routines	Movement disorders
Thalamus & Mammillary Bodies	Relay and recall in memory circuit	Korsakoff's syndrome

3. Memory Encoding, Storage, and Retrieval

This is the foundational process by which memory works in the brain. Think of it as a computer system with **input (encoding)**, **saving (storage)**, and **opening files (retrieval)**.

Encoding

- **Definition**: The process of converting sensory input (what we see, hear, feel, etc.) into a form the brain can use.

- **Types of encoding**:
    - **Visual Encoding** – images (e.g., remembering a face)
    - **Acoustic Encoding** – sounds (e.g., learning a song)
    - **Semantic Encoding** – meaning-based (e.g., understanding a concept)
- **Physiological Aspect**:
    - Involves **neuronal activation** and the beginning of **synaptic changes**.
    - **Hippocampus** and **prefrontal cortex** are active during encoding.

Storage

- **Definition**: The process of maintaining encoded information over time.
- **Levels**:
    - **Short-Term Storage** (in prefrontal cortex)
        - Temporary; lasts seconds to minutes.
        - Limited capacity (7±2 items, as per Miller).
    - **Long-Term Storage** (hippocampus and cortex)
        - Relatively permanent.
        - Depends on **synaptic consolidation** and **neuroplasticity**.
- **Memory consolidation**:
    - Process by which memories become stable in the brain.
    - Involves **sleep**, **rehearsal**, and **protein synthesis**.

Retrieval

- **Definition**: Accessing stored memories when needed.

- **Types**:
    - **Recall** – retrieving without cues (e.g., essay writing)
    - **Recognition** – identifying from choices (e.g., MCQs)
- **Brain Areas**: Prefrontal cortex, hippocampus
- **Cue-dependent**: Retrieval can improve with related cues (e.g., context, emotions)

4. Physiological and Neural Basis of Memory

This section explains *how brain cells physically change* to make memory possible — at the **cellular and molecular level**.

Synaptic Plasticity

- **Definition**: The brain's ability to change the strength of connections between neurons (synapses) based on experience.
- **Why it matters**: Learning and memory rely on forming or modifying these connections.

Long-Term Potentiation (LTP)

- **Definition**: A **long-lasting strengthening** of synapses based on recent activity.
- **Occurs mainly in**: Hippocampus, especially in pathways like *Schaffer Collaterals*
- **Mechanism**:
    - Repeated stimulation → Increased synaptic efficiency
    - More neurotransmitter release and receptor sensitivity (especially **NMDA and AMPA** glutamate receptors)
- **Analogy**: Like carving a deeper path in sand by running water through it again and again.

Long-Term Depression (LTD)

- **Definition**: A **weakening** of synapses due to lack of stimulation or reverse pattern of firing.
- **Function**: Helps remove outdated/unnecessary memories and make room for new learning.

Neurotransmitters Involved in Memory

1. Acetylcholine

- Key in **attention, learning, and memory**
- Deficits are associated with **Alzheimer's disease**
- Found in **hippocampus and cerebral cortex**

2. Glutamate

- **Primary excitatory neurotransmitter** in the brain
- Crucial for **LTP** and synaptic plasticity
- Activates **NMDA receptors**, essential for forming long-term memories

3. Dopamine

- Involved in **reward-based learning and motivation**
- Reinforces **emotional memory**, especially in limbic areas (e.g., amygdala, nucleus accumbens)
- Important in **working memory and goal-directed behaviour**

Role of Protein Synthesis in Memory Consolidation

- **Long-term memory** (not short-term) requires **new proteins** to stabilize synaptic changes.
- Occurs in:
    - **Dendritic spines** of neurons
    - **Cell bodies** for gene transcription (e.g., CREB protein pathway)
- Blocking protein synthesis (experimentally) disrupts the formation of long-term memories.
- **Memory consolidation** during **sleep** also involves this process.

6. Memory disorders & brain damage

Understanding memory disorders helps students grasp **how different brain regions contribute to memory,** and how damage or degeneration affects cognitive functioning.

1. Anterograde Amnesia

- **Definition**: Inability to form **new long-term memories** after the onset of damage.

- **Cause**: Often results from damage to the **hippocampus** or medial temporal lobe.

- **Short-Term Memory (STM)** is typically intact, but **consolidation into Long-Term Memory (LTM)** is impaired.

- **Famous Case**: **Patient H.M. (Henry Molaison)** – underwent bilateral hippocampal removal; could remember events before surgery but could not form new explicit memories afterward.

- **Example**: A person may have a conversation and forget it within minutes.

2. Retrograde Amnesia

- **Definition**: Inability to **recall past memories**, particularly those formed **before** a traumatic event or injury.

- **Cause**: Can result from head trauma, stroke, or damage to the **frontal or temporal lobes**.

- Often affects **episodic memory** (personal experiences) more than semantic memory (general knowledge).

- **Memory Recovery**: Sometimes memories are regained slowly in reverse order (newest forgotten, oldest retained).

- **Example**: A person may forget their wedding day but remember their childhood.

3. Alzheimer's Disease

- **Definition**: A progressive **neurodegenerative disorder** that affects memory, thinking, and behaviour.

- **Causes and Mechanisms**:
  - **Beta-amyloid plaques**: Clumps of protein outside neurons
  - **Neurofibrillary tangles**: Twisted fibers of **tau protein** inside neurons
  - **Neurotransmitter deficits**, especially **acetylcholine**

- **Brain Areas Affected**:
  - Early stages: **Hippocampus** (affects recent memory)
  - Later stages: **Cerebral cortex** (language, reasoning, motor functions)

- **Symptoms**:
  - Forgetting recent events or conversations

- o   Getting lost, repeating questions, confusion
- o   Eventually leads to **severe dementia**
- **Diagnosis**: Brain imaging, cognitive testing, and postmortem analysis

4. Korsakoff's Syndrome

- **Definition**: A chronic memory disorder linked to **vitamin B1 (thiamine) deficiency**, often associated with **long-term alcoholism**.
- **Causes**:
  - o   Severe malnutrition
  - o   Alcohol interferes with thiamine absorption and storage
- **Brain Areas Affected**:
  - o   **Mammillary bodies**
  - o   **Thalamus**
  - o   **Frontal lobes**
- **Symptoms**:
  - o   **Severe anterograde amnesia**
  - o   **Retrograde amnesia**
  - o   **Confabulation**: Fabricating stories to fill memory gaps
  - o   Lack of insight and apathy
- **Treatment**: Thiamine replacement and cessation of alcohol may stop progression, but damage is often irreversible if untreated.

Learning

1. Neurobiological Foundations of Learning

This area focuses on how the brain and its structures, chemicals, and plasticity mechanisms allow us to acquire, store, and retrieve new information or behaviours. Learning is not just a psychological phenomenon—it's rooted in neural activity and biological change.

a. Role of the Brain in Learning

Different brain regions contribute uniquely to learning types and memory formation:

1. **Hippocampus:**

   - Function: Crucial for forming and consolidating new declarative (explicit) memories, such as facts and events.

   - Example: When you remember a new psychology theory you just studied, the hippocampus is involved.

   - Also important in spatial learning (e.g., navigating environments).

2. **Amygdala:**

   - Function: Encodes emotional aspects of learning, especially fear and threat-related conditioning.

   - Example: Learning to avoid a place that caused stress or fear.

   - Strong emotions can enhance memory consolidation via amygdala-hippocampus interaction.

3. **Cerebellum:**

   - Function: Plays a role in motor learning and procedural memory (learning physical skills).

   - Example: Learning to ride a bicycle or type on a keyboard.

   - Involved in classical conditioning (e.g., eye-blink response).

4. **Prefrontal Cortex:**

   - Function: Supports attention, working memory, decision-making, and planning—crucial for goal-directed learning.

   - Example: Using logic to solve a problem or making a decision based on learned consequences.

   - It integrates information from multiple brain areas and plays a role in higher-order learning.

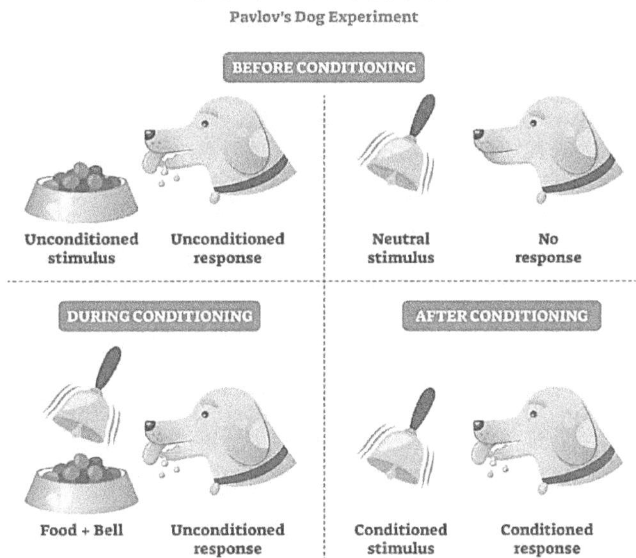

b. Neural Plasticity and Long-Term Potentiation (LTP)

1. Neural Plasticity:

- Definition: The brain's ability to change its structure and function in response to experience.
- Types: Structural (growth of new neurons/synapses) and functional (strengthening or weakening of synapses).
- Importance: Without plasticity, the brain couldn't adapt or form new memories.

2. Long-Term Potentiation (LTP):

- Definition: A long-lasting increase in synaptic strength following high-frequency stimulation of a synapse.
- Mechanism: Involves glutamate binding to NMDA receptors, calcium influx, and changes in the postsynaptic neuron.
- Role: Considered one of the primary cellular mechanisms underlying learning and memory.
- Location: Commonly studied in the hippocampus.

c. Neurotransmitters Involved in Learning

1. Dopamine:

- Role: Motivation, reinforcement learning, and reward-based learning.

- Example: Dopamine surges when you achieve a goal or are rewarded for an action, strengthening the behaviour.

2. Glutamate:

- Role: Primary excitatory neurotransmitter; essential for LTP and synaptic plasticity.

- Works through NMDA and AMPA receptors—key for learning-related changes at the synapse.

3. Acetylcholine (ACh):

- Role: Enhances attention, learning speed, and encoding of memories.

- Found in high concentrations in the hippocampus and neocortex.

- Deficits in ACh are linked with learning impairments and Alzheimer's disease.

4. Serotonin:

- Role: Modulates mood and indirectly supports learning, especially through regulating emotional states and impulsivity.

- Also involved in synaptic plasticity and some forms of non-associative learning (like habituation).

2. Types of Learning and Associated Brain Systems (Detailed)

1. Classical Conditioning (Pavlovian Conditioning)

This is a form of associative learning where a neutral stimulus becomes associated with a meaningful stimulus, producing a conditioned response.

Example: Pavlov's dog salivating to a bell after repeated bell-food pairings.

Introduced by:

Ivan Pavlov, a Russian physiologist, in the early 1900s.

Core Idea:

Learning through **association** – when two stimuli are repeatedly paired, an organism begins to associate them and responds to one as if it were the other.

Components:

Component	Description
Unconditioned Stimulus (UCS)	Naturally and automatically triggers a response (e.g., food).

Unconditioned Response (UCR)	Natural reaction to UCS (e.g., salivation to food).
Neutral Stimulus (NS)	A stimulus that initially produces no specific response (e.g., a bell).
Conditioned Stimulus (CS)	Former NS that, after association with UCS, triggers a response.
Conditioned Response (CR)	Learned response to the CS (e.g., salivation to bell).

Pavlov's Experiment:

- UCS: Food

- UCR: Salivation

- NS: Bell sound

- After repeated pairings (bell + food), the **bell alone** became the CS, and salivation became the CR.

Processes in Classical Conditioning:

Process	Description
Acquisition	Initial learning of the stimulus-response relationship.
Extinction	CR weakens when CS is repeatedly presented without the UCS.
Spontaneous Recovery	Reappearance of an extinguished CR after a rest period.
Generalization	Responding similarly to stimuli that resemble the CS (e.g., other bells).
Discrimination	Learning to distinguish between similar but different stimuli.

Neural Basis:

- **Cerebellum**: Crucial in the timing and coordination of conditioned motor responses. For instance, in eyeblink conditioning, the cerebellum plays a central role.

- **Amygdala**: Especially involved when the conditioned stimulus is emotionally charged, such as in fear conditioning. It processes emotional salience and links neutral stimuli with emotional outcomes.

Summary:
The cerebellum encodes the motor aspects of learned responses, while the amygdala is key in emotional conditioning.

2. Operant Conditioning (Instrumental Learning)

This learning depends on the consequences of behaviour — rewards reinforce behaviour, while punishments decrease its frequency.

Example: A rat presses a lever to get food (positive reinforcement).

Operant Conditioning (Instrumental Conditioning)

B.F. Skinner (built on Edward Thorndike's Law of Effect)

Core Idea:

Learning occurs through **consequences** – behaviours are strengthened or weakened based on the results they produce.

Skinner's Box:

Skinner used a chamber with levers or buttons that animals (e.g., rats or pigeons) could operate to obtain rewards (like food) or avoid punishment (like electric shocks).

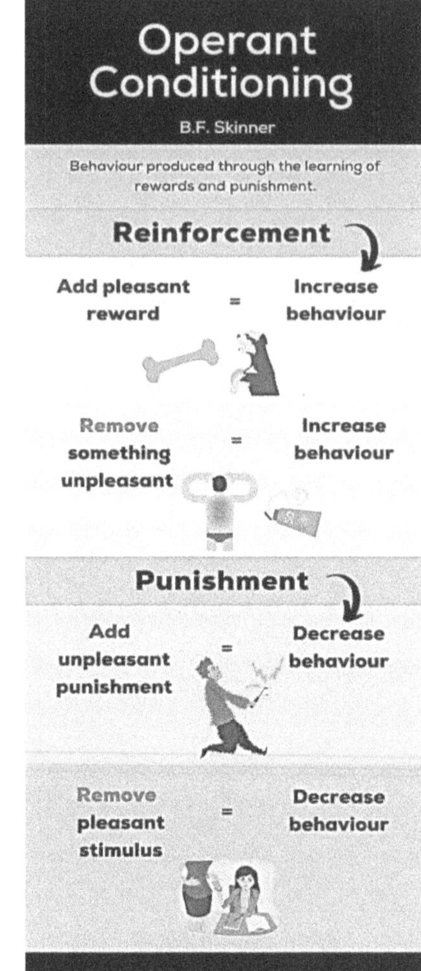

Key Concepts:

Term	Description
Reinforcement	Any consequence that **increases** the likelihood of a behaviour.
+ Positive Reinforcement	Adding something pleasant (e.g., giving a treat for good behaviour).
– Negative Reinforcement	Removing something unpleasant (e.g., turning off a loud noise when the behaviour is performed).
Punishment	Any consequence that **decreases** the likelihood of a behaviour.
+ Positive Punishment	Adding something unpleasant (e.g., scolding for misbehaviour).
– Negative Punishment	Taking away something pleasant (e.g., removing privileges).
Shaping	Gradually reinforcing successive steps toward a desired behaviour.
Extinction	When a behaviour decreases because it is no longer reinforced.

Schedules of Reinforcement:

Schedule Type	Description	Example
Fixed Ratio (FR)	Reinforcement after a fixed number of responses	Reward every 5th response
Variable Ratio (VR)	Reinforcement after a varying number of responses (most resistant to extinction)	Slot machines
Fixed Interval (FI)	Reinforcement after a fixed time interval	Weekly paycheck
Variable Interval (VI)	Reinforcement at unpredictable time intervals	Checking social media notifications

3. Law of Effect (by Edward Thorndike)

Core Principle:

Thorndike's Law of Effect states:

"Responses that produce a satisfying effect in a particular situation become more likely to occur again, and responses that produce a discomforting effect become less likely to occur again."

It is the basis for operant conditioning:

- **Satisfying outcome = Behaviour strengthened**

- **Unpleasant outcome = Behaviour weakened**

Neural Basis:

- **Basal Ganglia** (especially the striatum): Involved in learning the association between a behaviour and its outcome. Helps in habit formation.

- **Dopaminergic System**: Dopamine neurons in the ventral tegmental area (VTA) and substantia nigra play a key role in reinforcement learning. They signal reward prediction error — the difference between expected and received reward.

Summary:
Operant learning relies on dopamine-based reward signaling and motor circuits of the basal ganglia for shaping goal-directed behaviour.

3. Observational Learning (Modeling or Imitation)

This type involves learning by watching others, also called social learning.

Example: A child learns to wave by observing a parent.

Neural Basis:

- **Mirror Neuron System**: Located in areas like the premotor cortex and inferior parietal lobule. These neurons fire both when a person performs an action and when they observe the same action performed by another.

- **Frontal-Parietal Network**: Integrates observed action with internal motor plans. The superior temporal sulcus (STS) also helps interpret intentions.

Summary:

Observational learning uses mirror neurons and associated networks to match external behaviour with internal representations, enabling imitation and empathy.

4. Habituation and Sensitization

These are the simplest forms of non-associative learning.

- **Habituation**: Decreased response to a repeated, benign stimulus.

- **Sensitization**: Increased response to a strong or noxious stimulus.

 Example: Stop noticing the ticking of a clock (habituation); heightened reaction to a loud bang after a stressful event (sensitization).

 Neural Basis:

- **Sensory and Motor Synapses**: Changes occur at the synaptic level in the reflex arc. For instance, in the Aplysia sea slug, habituation is due to decreased neurotransmitter release, while sensitization increases neurotransmitter release due to modulatory interneurons.

- **Spinal Cord & Brainstem**: In humans, these processes often involve lower brain centres for reflexive responses.

Summary:
These forms of learning are fundamental and involve synaptic efficiency changes without needing higher cognitive involvement.

5. Disorders Related to Learning

A. Biological Bases of Learning Disabilities

1. **Dyslexia**

   o   Involves structural and functional differences in the left temporoparietal cortex, which is critical for phonological processing.

   o   Reduced activation in regions like the angular gyrus and inferior frontal gyrus.

   o   Genetic links include DYX1C1 and KIAA0319 genes.

2. **ADHD (Attention Deficit Hyperactivity Disorder)**

   o   Characterized by dysfunction in the prefrontal cortex and its connections with the basal ganglia.

   o   Associated with dopamine dysregulation.

   o   Genes such as DRD4 and DAT1 are frequently implicated.

3. **Autism Spectrum Disorder (ASD)**

   o   Affects social learning and communication.

   o   Differences in synaptic pruning and connectivity; genes such as MECP2 and SHANK3 involved.

B. Effects of Brain Injury, Trauma, or Degenerative Disease

1. **Traumatic Brain Injury (TBI)**

o   Damage to the frontal and temporal lobes impairs working memory, attention, and the ability to form new memories.

o   Neuroinflammation can disrupt neurotransmitter balance and neurogenesis.

2. **Stroke**

o   Depending on the area affected, learning can be compromised due to loss of language function (Broca's or Wernicke's area), spatial processing, or memory systems.

3. **Alzheimer's Disease**

o   A progressive degenerative disorder affecting the hippocampus and cerebral cortex.

o   Hallmarks include beta-amyloid plaques and tau tangles that interfere with synaptic transmission and plasticity.

4. **Chronic Stress and PTSD**

o   Elevated cortisol levels shrink the hippocampus, impairing memory and learning.

o   Alters connectivity in the limbic system and prefrontal cortex.

In Summary:

- **Biological findings** provide crucial support for cognitive models by showing how brain regions and neurotransmitters are involved in cognitive processes like attention, memory, and learning.

- However, **biological evidence also challenges** cognitive models by revealing that learning involves more than just information processing—it includes neural changes, emotional states, and embodied interactions.

- **Embodied cognition** argues that cognition is not just confined to the brain but is deeply influenced by our body's interactions with the environment, and this has profound implications for how learning occurs.

- The **brain-behaviour relationship** emphasizes that learning involves a dynamic interaction between brain activity and motor behaviours, highlighting the importance of the body in shaping cognitive functions.

This integration of cognitive psychology with physiological findings opens up a holistic view of learning, where biological processes, cognition, emotion, and body states work together to shape how we learn and adapt.

Emotion

Definition of Emotion

Emotion can be understood as a complex psychological and physiological response to a variety of stimuli, both internal and external. These responses are crucial for survival, decision-making, and maintaining social bonds.

- **Psychological Response**: This refers to the internal experience of emotions, such as feelings of happiness, sadness, anger, or fear. Emotions are often accompanied by a change in an individual's thoughts, perspectives, and mental state.

- **Physiological Response**: Emotions also trigger various physical changes in the body. These can range from heart rate increase, skin temperature change, breathing patterns, to hormonal fluctuations. These physical reactions are closely tied to how emotions are experienced and can be automatic or involuntary.

- **Survival Function**: Emotions are adaptive responses that have evolved to aid in survival. For example, fear prompts individuals to avoid danger, while joy encourages behaviours that foster social bonding and positive reinforcement.

- **Decision-Making**: Emotions play a significant role in decision-making by influencing judgments, actions, and priorities. Positive emotions can lead to risk-taking or exploration, while negative emotions may lead to caution or avoidance.

- **Social Bonding**: Emotions are key to social interactions and relationships. For instance, love, empathy, and compassion help strengthen social connections, while anger or jealousy can lead to conflict or social distancing.

Components of Emotion

1. Physiological Responses

When we experience an emotion, our body responds physiologically. These are automatic and largely governed by the autonomic nervous system (ANS). Emotions trigger the body's fight-or-flight or rest-and-digest responses.

- **Heart Rate**: Fear or excitement can elevate the heart rate as part of the body's readiness for action (e.g., fight or flight response).

- **Breathing**: During stress or fear, breathing tends to become faster and more shallow (sympathetic response), while relaxation or calmness brings deeper, slower breathing (parasympathetic response).

- **Muscle Tension**: Emotional states like anger or anxiety can cause increased muscle tension. The body prepares for a physical response, such as confronting a threat or fleeing from it.

- **Hormonal Fluctuations**: Emotions can cause changes in hormone levels. For instance, stress results in the release of cortisol, while happiness or love may increase oxytocin levels. Adrenaline is released during fear and excitement, preparing the body to react quickly.

2. Behavioural Responses

These are the external manifestations of emotions that can be seen or heard by others. Emotional expressions often involve a combination of facial expressions, body movements, posture, and vocal tone.

- **Facial Expressions**: The face is highly expressive, with emotions like happiness (smiling), anger (furrowed brows, clenched jaw), sadness (downturned mouth), and fear (wide eyes) showing distinct expressions.

- **Body Language**: Body posture and gestures also signal emotions. For instance, slouched shoulders can indicate sadness or defeat, while standing tall might reflect confidence or happiness. Open body posture is often associated with trust, while crossed arms can indicate defensiveness or discomfort.

- **Vocal Tone**: The way we speak also expresses our emotions. A shaky voice can reflect nervousness or fear, while a calm, steady voice typically suggests relaxation or contentment. The volume and pitch of speech can also change with emotional states (e.g., shouting when angry).

3. Cognitive Appraisal

Cognitive appraisal is the process by which we interpret and evaluate the significance of a situation, which in turn triggers an emotional response. It's the personal interpretation of events that affects how we feel about them.

- **Primary Appraisal**: This involves evaluating whether a situation is relevant to your well-being, and whether it's threatening or benign. For example, if you're walking in the woods and see a snake, your primary appraisal would assess if the snake is a threat (e.g., poisonous).

- **Secondary Appraisal**: After evaluating the situation, individuals assess their ability to cope with it. If a person feels they have the resources (e.g., ability to escape), their emotional response may be less intense. In contrast, if they feel helpless, they may experience heightened fear or anxiety.

- **Example**: The feeling of fear upon seeing a snake is not only because of the snake itself but because of the cognitive evaluation of its potential danger. If an individual perceives the snake as harmless (secondary appraisal), they may experience curiosity rather than fear.

4. Subjective Experience

This is the internal, personal, and qualitative aspect of emotions. The subjective experience refers to the feelings or "what it's like" to experience an emotion. These emotions often arise as a result of both cognitive appraisal and physiological changes.

- **Sadness**: When feeling sad, a person may experience a heavy, downcast feeling, a sense of loss or disappointment, and an overall sense of emotional numbness. This is subjective, and each person may experience sadness differently.

- **Joy**: The feeling of joy can manifest as a sense of lightness, happiness, or exhilaration. People often feel a sense of energy and satisfaction.

- **Anger**: Anger can feel like an intense surge of heat or tension in the body, accompanied by thoughts of injustice or frustration. It can feel consuming or overwhelming to those experiencing it.

- **Fear**: The subjective experience of fear often involves a heightened state of alertness, a sense of urgency, and sometimes an inability to think clearly. It may feel like a freeze or flight response, with physical sensations of dread or tension.

Integration of Components

All these components of emotion—physiological, behavioural, cognitive, and subjective—are interconnected and interact to create a full emotional experience. For example, when you feel anger:

- Your body experiences physiological changes (increased heart rate, tension).

- You might express anger through body language (clenched fists, frown) or vocal tone (shouting).

- You cognitively appraise the situation as unfair or threatening.

- Subjectively, you feel a surge of frustration or rage.

1. James-Lange Theory of Emotion

Overview: This is one of the earliest theories of emotion, proposed by **William James** and **Carl Lange** in the late 19th century. It posits that emotions are the result of our body's physiological reactions to external stimuli.

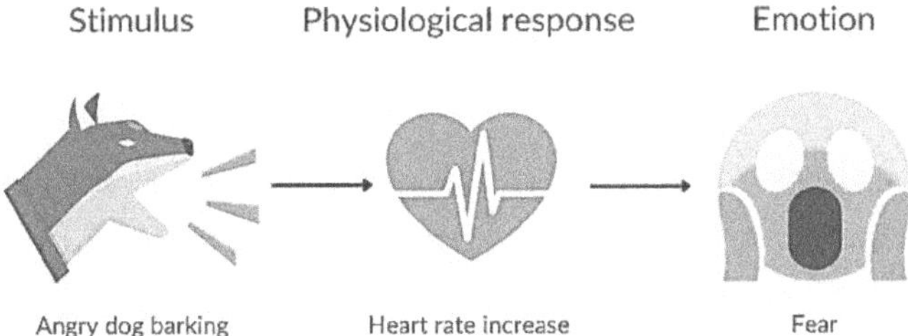

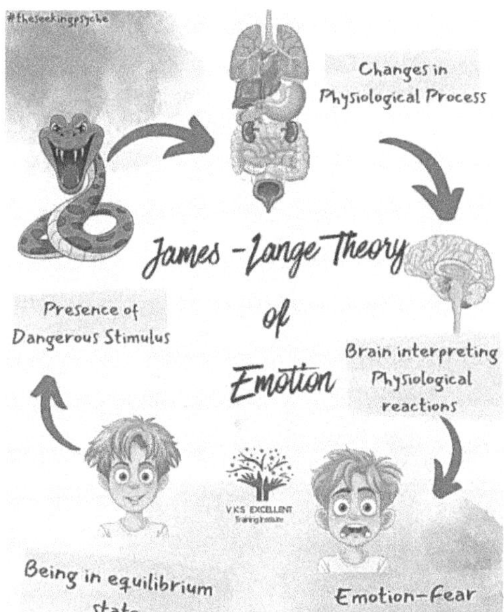

Key Concept: According to this theory, **we feel emotions because we experience bodily changes**. The physiological changes (like an increase in heart rate or muscle tension) occur first, and then the brain interprets these changes as specific emotions.**Example**: Imagine you're walking in a dark alley and suddenly see a shadow. According to James-Lange, the **fear you experience** comes from your **physical response** to the situation, such as your heart racing or your hands trembling. You interpret these physical sensations, and then you label it as **fear**.

Criticism: A major criticism of this theory is that it assumes that every emotion has a unique physiological response. However, many emotions (e.g., fear, excitement) have similar bodily responses, making it difficult to distinguish between them based purely on physical changes.

2. Cannon-Bard Theory of Emotion

Overview: This theory was proposed by **Walter Cannon** and **Philip Bard** as a challenge to the James-Lange Theory. According to Cannon-Bard, emotions are not simply the result of physiological reactions, but rather **emotions and physiological responses occur simultaneously** in response to an external stimulus.

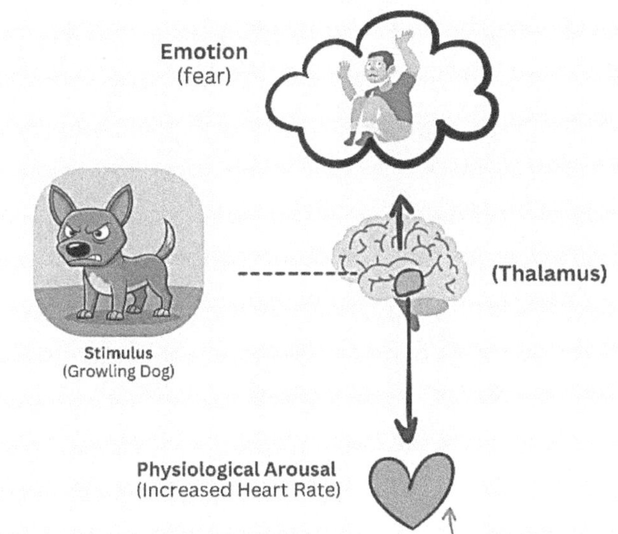

Key Concept: Cannon-Bard proposed that when an emotional stimulus is perceived, it is processed by the brain, and both the emotional experience and the bodily reaction (like increased heart rate) occur **at the same time**. Therefore, the emotional experience is not the consequence of the physiological reaction, but both happen **simultaneously**.

Example: In the same scenario where you encounter the shadow in the dark alley, **both the emotional feeling of fear** and the **physiological reaction** (such as increased heart rate and sweating) happen at the same time. The brain simultaneously processes the emotional response and sends signals to the body.

Criticism: One challenge to this theory is that it doesn't fully explain how **the body's physical response** influences emotions. It doesn't fully account for the fact that the body does play a role in how we experience emotions.

3. Schachter-Singer Two-Factor Theory of Emotion

Overview: Proposed by **Stanley Schachter** and **Jerome Singer** in 1962, this theory builds on both the **James-Lange Theory** and the **Cannon-Bard Theory**. It suggests that emotions are a result of two factors: **physiological arousal** and **cognitive labeling** of that arousal.

Key Concept: The theory posits that when we experience **physiological arousal** (e.g., increased heart rate, sweating), we don't automatically know what emotion we are feeling. Instead, we look for a **cognitive explanation** for that arousal, which leads us to label our experience as a particular emotion (like fear, excitement, or anger).

Example: Let's say you're walking in the dark alley again, and you feel your heart rate increasing and your

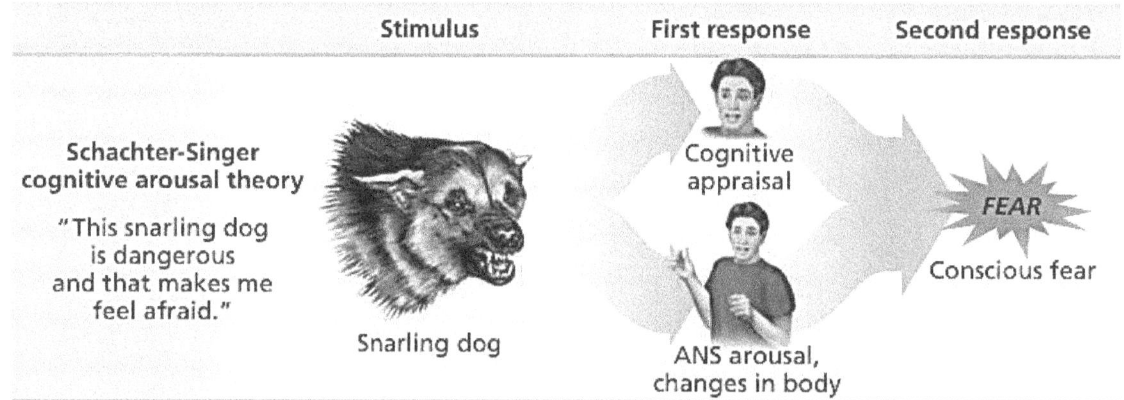

palms sweating. According to the Schachter-Singer theory, **the physiological response** (the arousal) alone doesn't define the emotion. You might look around and see the shadowy figure, and you **label** your arousal as **fear**. If you were in a different situation, perhaps on a thrilling roller coaster, the same physiological arousal could be labeled as **excitement**.

Criticism: The theory is praised for integrating both the physiological and cognitive aspects of emotions, but it has been critiqued for the **vagueness** in how we cognitively label and interpret physiological states. It can be difficult to explain why we label some emotions one way and others differently in similar situations.

4. Lazarus Cognitive-Mediational Theory of Emotion

Overview: Proposed by **Richard Lazarus** in the 1960s, this theory emphasizes the **role of cognitive appraisal** in the experience of emotions. According to Lazarus, emotions arise from how we **interpret or appraise a situation**, which then leads to both physiological and emotional responses.

Key Concept: Unlike the James-Lange theory, which suggests emotions follow physiological reactions, Lazarus argues that emotions begin with our **interpretation (appraisal)** of an event. The way we **evaluate the significance** of the event determines the emotional response we will experience. The emotional experience and the bodily response are shaped by our **appraisal**.

Stimulus | First response | Second response

Lazarus's cognitive-mediational theory

"The snarling dog is dangerous and therefore I should feel afraid."

Appraisal of threat — FEAR — Bodily response

There are two types of appraisal in Lazarus' theory:

- **Primary Appraisal**: We first assess whether an event is **irrelevant**, **benign-positive**, or **harmful** (a threat or challenge).

- **Secondary Appraisal**: We then assess whether we have the **resources** to cope with the situation.

Example: If you're walking in the dark alley and see the shadow, your **primary appraisal** might determine if you view it as a threat (danger) or just a harmless object. If you perceive it as dangerous, your **secondary appraisal** will assess whether you can defend yourself. The **emotion** you feel (fear, anxiety) and your **physiological response** (e.g., increased heart rate, tension) depend on these appraisals.

Criticism: While this theory highlights the **importance of cognitive processes**, it may not fully account for emotions that arise without conscious thought or appraisal (like automatic emotional responses).

Summary:

Stimulus
First response
Second response

Common sense theory
"I'm shaking because I'm afraid."
Snarling dog
FEAR
Conscious fear
ANS arousal

James-Lange theory
"I'm afraid because I'm shaking."
Snarling dog
ANS arousal, changes in body
FEAR
Conscious fear

Cannon-Bard theory
"I'm shaking and feeling afraid at the same time."
Snarling dog
Subcortical brain activity
ANS arousal, changes in body
FEAR
Conscious fear

Schachter-Singer cognitive arousal theory
"This snarling dog is dangerous and that makes me feel afraid."
Snarling dog
Cognitive appraisal
ANS arousal, changes in body
FEAR
Conscious fear

Facial feedback theory
"The fearful expression on my face enhances my sense of being afraid."
ANS arousal in face
Facial expression
Cognitive interpretation of face motions
FEAR

Lazarus's cognitive-mediational theory
"The snarling dog is dangerous and therefore I should feel afraid."
Appraisal of threat
FEAR
Bodily response

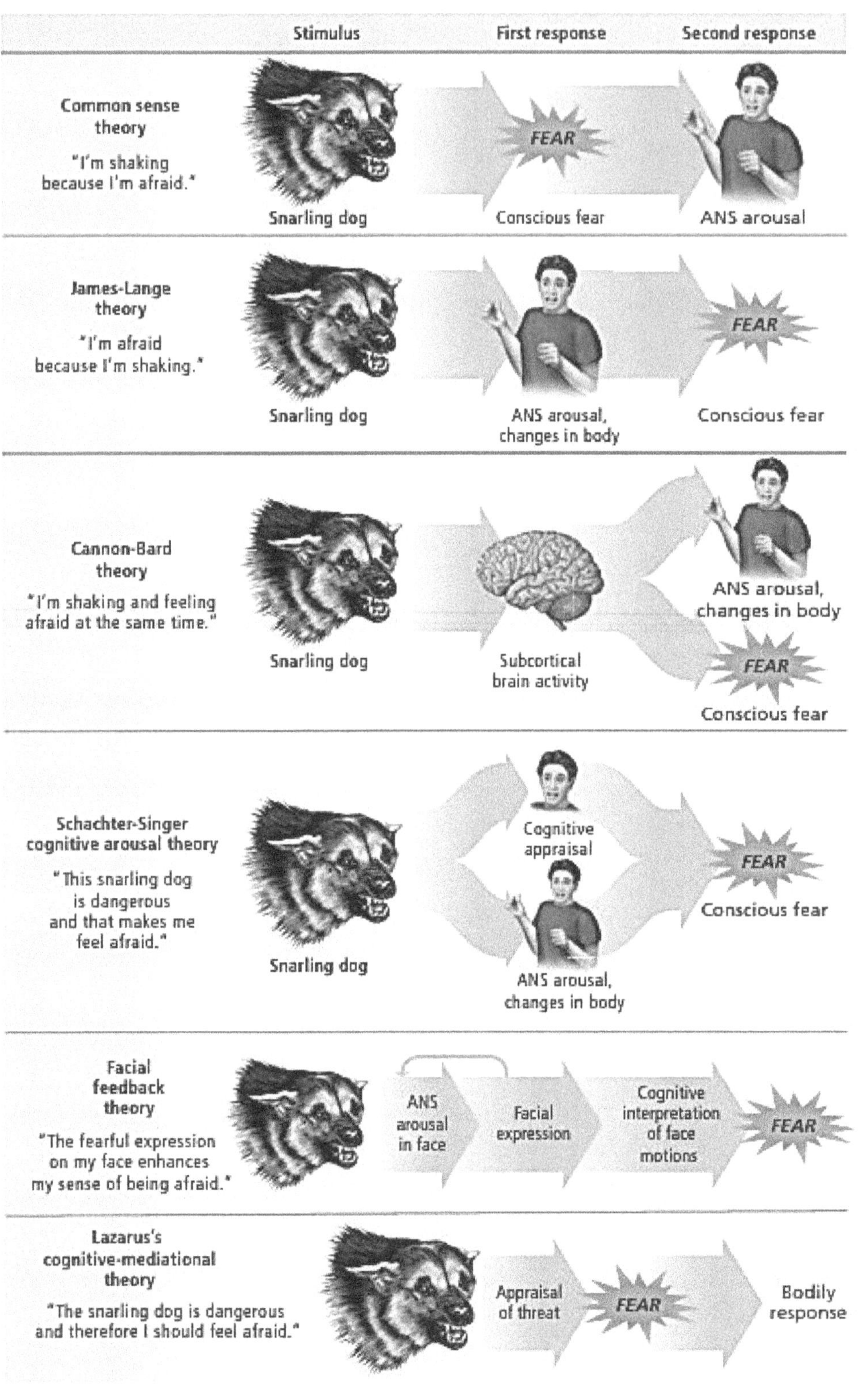

- **James-Lange**: Emotions are a result of physiological responses to stimuli.

- **Cannon-Bard**: Emotions and physiological responses happen simultaneously.

- **Schachter-Singer**: Emotions depend on both physiological arousal and cognitive interpretation.

- **Lazarus**: Emotions are based on cognitive appraisals (interpretations) of a situation.

1. The Role of the Brain in Emotions

Emotions are intricately tied to specific brain structures, and different brain regions contribute to the experience and regulation of emotions in different ways. Here's how key parts of the brain contribute to emotions:

The Limbic System

The limbic system is often referred to as the "emotional brain," and it plays a central role in regulating emotions. Major structures involved include:

- **Amygdala**: This almond-shaped structure is crucial for processing emotions, particularly **fear** and **anger**. It helps detect threats and triggers appropriate physiological responses. The amygdala is involved in forming emotional memories, which can influence how emotions are experienced in future situations. For example, a person who has experienced trauma may have a hyperactive amygdala, which makes them more sensitive to fear-inducing stimuli.

- **Hypothalamus**: The hypothalamus regulates the **autonomic nervous system** and is responsible for controlling basic bodily functions, such as heart rate and respiration. It connects emotional experiences to physiological responses. For instance, when a person experiences stress, the hypothalamus triggers the release of cortisol, a stress hormone, activating the **fight-or-flight** response.

- **Hippocampus**: Though primarily involved in memory, the hippocampus helps link emotional experiences with memories, shaping future emotional responses. It works closely with the amygdala to modulate emotional intensity based on past experiences.

Prefrontal Cortex

The **prefrontal cortex (PFC)** is the brain's executive center and plays a critical role in **emotion regulation**. It is involved in higher-order functions such as decision-making, impulse control, and self-regulation. It helps individuals assess emotional situations and decide how to respond, sometimes overriding emotional impulses to make more reasoned decisions. For example, the PFC may suppress emotional responses like anger in a social setting or help manage stress during high-pressure situations. It is also involved in cognitive strategies like **reappraisal** (reinterpreting an emotional situation to alter its impact) and **self-reflection**, which helps in emotional growth.

2. Brain Areas Involved in Different Emotions

Different emotions are processed in different regions of the brain:

- **Fear**: The amygdala plays a central role in the experience of fear. When a person perceives a threat, the amygdala triggers an immediate fear response. This might involve changes in heart rate, muscle tension, and heightened alertness.

- **Disgust**: The **insula**, located deep within the cerebral cortex, is activated when we experience disgust. This emotion is particularly strong in reactions to offensive smells, tastes, or visual stimuli.

- **Happiness**: The **ventral striatum** (including the nucleus accumbens) is involved in the experience of pleasure and reward. Dopamine release in this area is linked to feelings of happiness and reward.

- **Sadness**: The **anterior cingulate cortex** (ACC) is activated during emotional pain and sadness. It is believed to be involved in regulating the body's emotional and physiological responses to sadness, particularly in the context of loss or social rejection.

3. Autonomic Nervous System (ANS)

The autonomic nervous system (ANS) regulates involuntary bodily functions, and it plays a significant role in the physical manifestations of emotions. The ANS is divided into two branches:

- **Sympathetic Nervous System (SNS)**: Often called the "fight-or-flight" system, the SNS is activated in response to stressful or threatening situations. It increases heart rate, redirects blood flow to muscles, dilates the pupils, and prepares the body to respond to perceived danger. This is an **emotional response** to acute stress or fear.

- **Parasympathetic Nervous System (PNS)**: The PNS is responsible for the "rest-and-digest" functions, helping to calm the body after a stress response. It slows the heart rate, promotes digestion, and returns the body to a state of homeostasis. Emotional regulation, such as the calming effects after anger or anxiety, is largely mediated by the PNS.

4. Emotional Regulation

Emotional regulation refers to the processes by which individuals manage and modify their emotional responses, and it is influenced by both cognitive and physiological mechanisms:

- **Reappraisal**: This is a cognitive strategy in which an individual reinterprets a situation to alter its emotional impact. For example, rethinking a stressful situation as an opportunity for growth can reduce anxiety and stress.

- **Suppression**: Suppression involves inhibiting emotional expressions, such as trying to hide feelings of sadness or anger. While suppression can provide short-term relief, it can have long-term consequences on mental health and emotional well-being.

- **Mindfulness**: Being aware of and accepting one's emotions without judgment is a key aspect of emotional regulation. Mindfulness practices, such as meditation, can help reduce emotional reactivity and enhance emotional resilience.

5. Cultural and Social Aspects of Emotion

Emotions are not purely biological; they are also shaped by cultural and social influences:

- **Cultural Norms**: Different cultures have distinct norms about how emotions should be expressed and regulated. For example, in some cultures, it is acceptable to show emotional vulnerability, while in others, emotional restraint may be expected. These cultural norms can shape how people experience and display emotions.

- **Gender Differences**: Research suggests that societal expectations influence how men and women express emotions. For example, women may be socialized to express sadness more openly, while men may be encouraged to suppress emotional vulnerability and express anger instead.

- **Cultural Variations**: Some emotions are universally recognized (e.g., fear, happiness, sadness), but how they are experienced and expressed can vary widely across cultures. For example, the experience of shame may be more pronounced in collectivist societies, while individualist societies may focus more on pride and self-affirmation.

6. Neurotransmitters and Hormones

Emotions are closely tied to the release of various neurotransmitters and hormones, which mediate the physiological and psychological aspects of emotional experiences:

- **Serotonin**: Often referred to as the "feel-good" neurotransmitter, serotonin plays a role in regulating mood, anxiety, and emotional well-being. Low serotonin levels are associated with depression and emotional instability.

- **Dopamine**: Dopamine is central to the reward system and is associated with pleasure, motivation, and positive emotions. High levels of dopamine are linked to feelings of happiness and excitement, while low levels are connected to anhedonia (inability to experience pleasure).

- **Cortisol**: Cortisol is a hormone released in response to stress. It is vital for the body's fight-or-flight response, but chronic stress can lead to elevated cortisol levels, which can have negative impacts on mental and physical health, including increased anxiety and mood disorders.

- **Oxytocin**: Often called the "love hormone," oxytocin is released during social bonding activities such as hugging, childbirth, and breastfeeding. It promotes trust, empathy, and social connections, and it plays a role in regulating emotions like affection and attachment.

OTHER THEORIES THAT DESCRIBE ELICITATION OF EMOTIONS

1. Evolutionary Theory of Emotion:

The **Evolutionary Theory** of emotion suggests that emotions evolved because they were adaptive responses that enhanced survival and reproductive success. Emotions serve as mechanisms to help humans respond effectively to environmental challenges. They are believed to have developed over time because they played an essential role in helping individuals navigate the world, make decisions, and react to potential threats or opportunities.

- **Adaptive Value of Emotions**: According to this theory, emotions are innate and universal, designed to help humans survive in different environments. For example:

  o **Fear** triggers the body's fight-or-flight response, helping us react quickly to danger (e.g., running away from a predator).

  o **Disgust** helps us avoid harmful substances or situations that could lead to illness (e.g., avoiding spoiled food or toxic environments).

  o **Happiness** reinforces behaviours that are beneficial to survival, such as cooperation and social bonding, which help in creating supportive social groups.

- **Social Bonding**: Emotions like **love** and **compassion** promote social bonding and cooperation within groups, which are essential for survival in human societies. Early humans relied on group cooperation for hunting, protection, and resource-sharing. Emotions like **empathy** allowed for understanding others' feelings and creating strong social networks.

- **Emotional Expression**: The theory also explains why emotions are expressed in universally recognizable ways. For example, facial expressions of anger or fear are similar across cultures, supporting the idea that emotions are biologically programmed to serve survival functions.

2. Attachment Theory:

Attachment Theory, developed by **John Bowlby**, posits that early emotional bonds formed between a child and their primary caregiver (often the mother) have a profound influence on the child's emotional development and psychological well-being throughout life. These early attachments shape how individuals interact with others in later stages of life and influence their emotional functioning.

- **Attachment Behaviours**: In infancy, a child's attachment behaviours are geared towards maintaining proximity to the caregiver for survival and protection. A secure attachment leads to feelings of safety and comfort, while an insecure attachment can result in anxiety and mistrust.

- **Types of Attachment**:

  o **Secure Attachment**: Children who develop a secure attachment to their caregivers feel safe to explore the world, knowing they can return to the caregiver for comfort. This leads to a healthy emotional and social development.

- Insecure Attachment: Children with inconsistent or neglectful caregivers may develop **anxious**, **avoidant**, or **disorganized** attachment styles, which can lead to difficulties in forming stable and trusting relationships later in life. These individuals might experience anxiety, difficulty with intimacy, or avoidance in relationships.

- **Impact on Adult Relationships**: Attachment styles formed in childhood influence adult relationships. For example, individuals with a secure attachment style tend to have healthier relationships, characterized by trust and emotional regulation. In contrast, those with insecure attachment may struggle with emotional regulation, trust, and maintaining relationships.

- **Emotional Regulation**: Attachment theory also ties into emotional regulation. Securely attached children learn to manage their emotions because they can rely on their caregiver's comforting responses. On the other hand, insecure attachments can hinder emotional regulation, resulting in difficulties in handling emotions like anxiety or sadness.

3. Cognitive-Behavioural Perspective:

The **Cognitive-Behavioural Perspective** (CBT) suggests that emotions are deeply influenced by our thought patterns, beliefs, and cognitive biases. According to this approach, our emotional experiences arise from the way we interpret events, not from the events themselves. CBT emphasizes that by changing maladaptive thought patterns, individuals can improve their emotional regulation and behaviour.

- **Cognitive Appraisal**: The way we appraise or interpret a situation determines how we feel emotionally. For example, if someone perceives a situation as threatening or overwhelming, they are more likely to feel anxiety or fear. If they see it as a challenge they can handle, they might feel excited or motivated. This cognitive appraisal of events heavily influences emotional responses.

- **Cognitive Distortions**: These are irrational or biased ways of thinking that can lead to negative emotional states. Common cognitive distortions include:

- Catastrophizing: Expecting the worst possible outcome (e.g., thinking, "If I fail this exam, my life will be ruined").

- **All-or-Nothing Thinking**: Seeing situations in black-and-white terms, without acknowledging any middle ground (e.g., "If I make a mistake, I'm a complete failure").

- **Overgeneralization**: Making broad conclusions based on a single event (e.g., "I failed one test, so I'm not smart enough for college").

These thought patterns can lead to negative emotions like anxiety, depression, or anger.

- **Behavioural Responses**: The thoughts we have can also influence how we behave. For example, if someone believes that they are incapable of succeeding (due to negative thoughts), they might avoid trying new things, which can reinforce feelings of helplessness and further perpetuate emotional distress.

- **Cognitive-Behavioural Therapy (CBT)**: This therapeutic approach is based on the premise that by identifying and challenging negative or distorted thought patterns, individuals can improve their emotional responses and behaviours. For example, by recognizing and challenging catastrophic thoughts, a person can reduce anxiety and improve their ability to cope with stress.